Bricks, Pavers & Tiles

Bricks, Pavers & Tiles

FRANK GARDNER,
DIETER MYLIUS, SABINA ROBBA
& JOHN STREET

MURDOCH
B O O K S

CONTENTS

TILING 132

Bricklaying

Bricks and blocks can be used in a wide variety of different ways in the garden – for walls, for steps and for paving. Here they are used with pavers, pebbles and gravel to creat interesting contrasts.

Bricks and bricklaying

Strong, attractive brickwork results from a careful choice of bricks and neat, precise bricklaying.

Most bricks used around the home are made from clay or shale fired in a kiln or oven. Calcium silicate bricks are made from sand or crushed flint and hardened under steam pressure whilst concrete bricks (referred to as 'blocks') are made from cement mixed with aggregates.

Bricks are made to a 'modular' size – 225 mm long, 112.5 mm thick and 75 mm high. This module includes one 10 mm mortar course, so that the actual size of the brick is 215 x 102.5 x 65 mm: two module thicknesses or three module heights equal one module length – an important relationship in bricklaying.

Bricks can be cut using a club hammer and bolster chisel. A half brick is known as a bat. The brick or block you choose for a project depends on its type, its variety and its quality. It may also be described by its colour or where it was made.

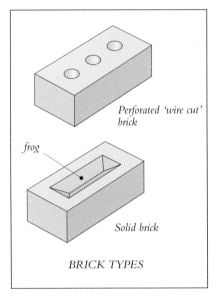

Perforated 'wire cut' brick

frog

Solid brick

BRICK TYPES

To cut bricks hold a bolster steady at the appropriate point and strike it firmly with a club hammer.

TYPES OF BRICK

• Solid bricks are the most familiar and often have a frog (a depression in one face) from the manufacturing process. They can be machine made (moulded or pressed) or hand made.

• Perforated bricks have holes running through the thickness (so vertical when laid). If the holes make up less than 25 per cent of the volume, the brick is classified as solid. Many perforated bricks are known as 'wirecut' as they are cut with a wire after being extruded though a die in the making process.

• Shaped bricks are for corners, sills and cappings (tops of walls).

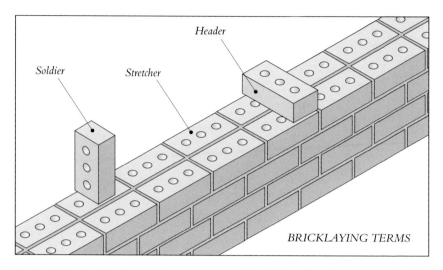

Header

Soldier *Stretcher*

BRICKLAYING TERMS

VARIETIES OF BRICK
The three common varieties of brick are used for different purposes.
• Common bricks are used for general building work, especially for walls which will later be plastered or rendered. Many common bricks are described as flettons.
• Facing bricks are used where they will be seen and have at least one acceptable face. Normally stronger and better quality than common bricks, they are used for garden walls and external house walls.
• Engineering bricks are very dense and are strong and resistant to moisture. This makes them suitable for use in retaining walls and for courses of wall below ground level.

BRICK QUALITIES
This refers to weather resistance.
• Ordinary bricks are suitable for the outside face of a building, but should be frost resistant if used in garden walls.

• Special quality bricks are durable even when soaking wet and are suitable for all garden walling, including retaining walls.
• Internal bricks are only suitable for walls inside the house.

CONCRETE BLOCKS
For garden walling, 'reconstituted stone' blocks are a popular choice. Made mainly from concrete, they give the appearance of natural stone. They come in single units (roughly the same size as a brick) and multiple units, the size of several bricks, with mortar courses already in place.

LAYING BRICKS
Bricks can be laid in different ways. The terms most often used are:
• stretcher – laid lengthwise in a wall;
• header – laid through a wall, at right angles to stretchers;
• soldier – stood on end or on edge (often used on the tops of walls).

TYPES OF BRICKS

Interlocking clay paver

Moulded stock facing brick

Clay paver

Hand-made stock facing brick

Extruded common brick

Sand-faced facing brick

Double bullnose brick for capping

'Reconstituted stone' concrete walling block

Multiple concrete walling block

Pierced screen walling block

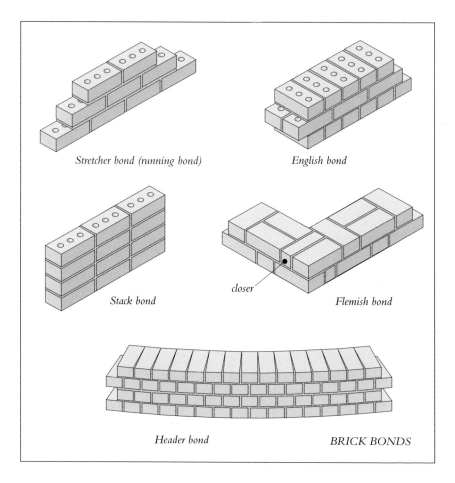

Stretcher bond (running bond)

English bond

Stack bond

closer

Flemish bond

Header bond

BRICK BONDS

BRICK BONDS

For maximum strength, successive layers (courses) of brick are lapped one over the other. This overlapping is known as bonding. Poor bonding can lead to weakness in a wall.

• In stretcher bond (running bond) all the bricks are laid as stretchers. Used for general construction work.

• In Flemish bond (another strong bond), each course consists of alternate headers and pairs of stretchers. Half-brick 'closers' are needed on each course.

• In English bond, alternate courses of bricks are laid as headers and stretchers. A very strong bond, it is often used for retaining walls.

• In stack bond the bricks are laid vertically on top of each other (the bricks must all be exactly the same size). This is a very weak bond and it is used only for feature panels or screen block walls.

• In header bond all the bricks are laid as headers. Most often used for circular walls or curved brickwork.

BRICKLAYING

Accuracy and neatness are very important in bricklaying. Brickwork must be checked frequently for plumb (vertical) and for level.

Keep the work area neat and tidy, free of broken bricks and old mortar, so you don't fall over them or dirty the new brickwork. Store bricks and sand close to the work site, and cover them to keep them dry. Store bags of cement and lime in a dry area.

CALCULATING THE NUMBER OF BRICKS

In order to build 1 m^2 of single-thickness brick wall you will need sixty bricks. To calculate how many bricks you will need for a wall, follow these steps:

1 Find the overall area of the wall to be built by multiplying the length by the height in metres.

2 Calculate the areas of any openings and subtract these from the overall area.

3 Multiply the area by 60 to find the number of bricks required for a single-thickness wall.

4 If the wall is to be two bricks thick, then multiply the overall area of the wall by 120.

MATCHING BRICKS AND MORTAR

When bricking up unwanted openings in brick walls or adding a new section of wall, you need to carefully match the existing bricks for size and texture. If the wall is to be left unpainted, you will also need to match the bricks for colour.

In the UK, bricks are now made to a metric format and the main size problem is matching new metric bricks to old imperial ones. The best chance will be to buy second-hand bricks from an architectural salvage yard, where you may also get a good match in texture and colour. If you cannot get matching bricks, increase the size of the mortar courses by 1.2 mm.

It can also be difficult to find the correct mix and colour for the mortar. The following is a rough guide to mortar colours (see also page 25). Experiment with the mix to get a precise match. Remember to let the new mix dry before comparing it with the existing mortar.

• White mortar. Use white sand, white cement and lime.
• Grey mortar. Use a mix of bricklayer's sand (loam colour) and grey cement.
• Red mortar. Use bricklayer's sand, grey cement and red oxide.
• Black mortar. Use bricklayer's sand, grey cement and black oxide.

Preparing the site

Careful setting out is the first step for any successful bricklaying project. You may need to consult a surveyor for large projects or those close to a boundary.

TOOLS AND MATERIALS

- Measuring tape
- Timber stakes
- Timber for profiles
- Nails and hammer
- String
- Spirit level
- Line level
- Plumb bob
- Builders square
- 12 mm clear tube water level
- Spade

SETTING OUT

Measure out the outline of your job and erect timber profiles about 1 m beyond the outline. This keeps them out of the way when you are digging the foundation trenches. Tie string lines to the nails in the profiles to indicate the width of the trench (see page 17) and walls to act as guides. Then sprinkle a line of lime exactly under the string line to provide a guide for digging.

When setting out trenches, ensure the corners are at right angles. Check with a builders square or use

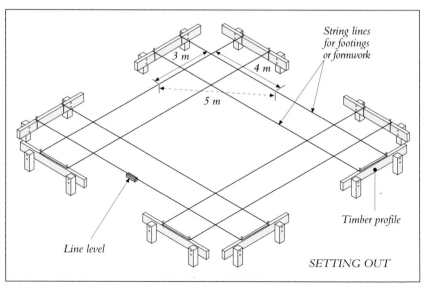

String lines for footings or formwork

3 m

4 m

5 m

Timber profile

Line level

SETTING OUT

Each panel of this high brick wall is stepped down so that the wall maintains an even height down the slope. Because the steps are large, the capping bricks are also stepped to achieve a more flowing effect.

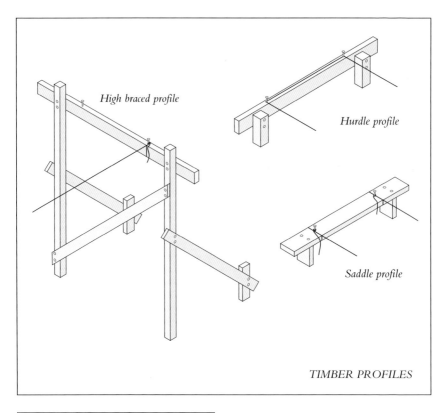

High braced profile

Hurdle profile

Saddle profile

TIMBER PROFILES

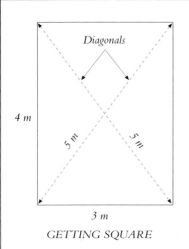

Diagonals

4 m

5 m

5 m

3 m

GETTING SQUARE

the 3-4-5 method (see the diagrams at left and on page 14). Measure along one side 3 m from the corner and then 4 m along the other side (or you can use any multiples of these

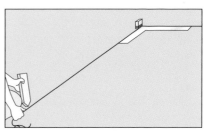

A builders square can be used to check the corners of the area are square when setting string lines.

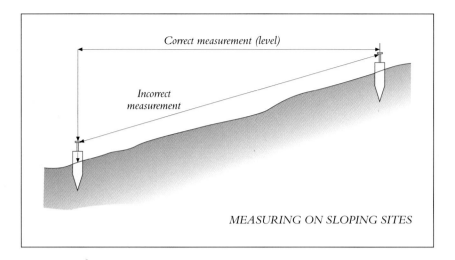

Correct measurement (level)

Incorrect measurement

MEASURING ON SLOPING SITES

numbers, for example, 300 and 400 mm, or 600 and 800 mm). The third side of the triangle should equal 5 m (or 500 mm or 1 m, as appropriate) if you have made a right angle.

When set out, check that all corners are square by checking the two diagonals are the same length. Measurements should always be taken on the level, even if you are on a sloping site. Use a spirit level to ensure the tape measure is level.

ESTABLISHING LEVELS

When setting out a project, establish levels accurately. Put a timber stake in the ground at each corner of the job. Mark near the top of one stake and mark the other stakes at the same height, using a 12 mm clear tube water level or a timber straight-edge (100 x 25 mm) and spirit level. Adjust each of the string lines to this level and check with a line level hooked on to each string in turn.

FOUNDATION TRENCHES

A single-thickness brick wall up to 750 mm high needs concrete foundations (footings) at least 350 mm wide and 150 mm deep; for double-thickness walls (up to 1.5 m high), use a width of 530 mm. On sites exposed to wind, increase the width by 50 mm; on soft (such as clay) soils, increase the depth by 75 mm.

To find the level for the top of the footings (which should be 150 or 225 mm below ground level), measure down an equal distance from the level mark on each stake. If the ground is not level you may have to step the footings. To make bricklaying easier, each step should be 75 or 150 mm (the height of one or two bricks plus mortar) so that you don't have to cut the bricks.

When digging, keep within the string lines. Keep the sides of the trench vertical and straight.

Concrete footings

Concrete footings are necessary to provide a firm base for a brick wall. Concrete can be mixed by hand, prepared using a concrete mixer or delivered to the site ready mixed.

TOOLS AND MATERIALS

- Timber for formwork
- Timber stakes, nails and hammer
- Steel reinforcement (mesh or bars, stirrups and bar chairs)
- Tie-wire and pliers
- Cement, sand and coarse aggregate
- Concrete mixer (hired)
- Wheelbarrow, shovel and gum boots
- Straight-edge and spirit level
- Steel and wooden floats

FORMWORK

Usually concrete is poured directly into the foundation trench but you may need to build formwork if the footing will rise above ground level.

Formwork is a temporary frame, usually made of timber or plywood, that holds concrete to the required shape until it has hardened. It must be well staked to withstand the pressure of the wet concrete.

Use long pieces of timber and hold them in place with stakes. Use a spirit level to check that the formwork is level.

SIZE OF TRENCHES

Footings are usually twice the width of the finished wall. If you are using formwork, allow 100 mm extra width for the frame and supporting stakes.

STEEL REINFORCEMENT

To give concrete strength and rigidity and prevent it bending under load, it can be reinforced with two layers of steel bars or trench mesh. The bars are tied to stirrups with wire and should overlap a minimum of 450 mm when they join. Place

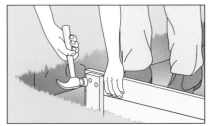

Use stakes to support the formwork and hold it in place. It must withstand the pressure of the concrete.

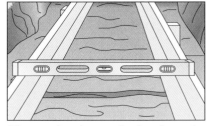

Use a level to check that the formwork is level. You will then be able to level off the concrete easily.

Concrete footings can be reinforced with steel bars or mesh. To hold them in position near the top and bottom of the concrete they are secured to stirrups, which can be suspended by wire from timber beams.

them as near the top and bottom of the concrete as possible (see page 20) and at least 60 mm from the edges. The stirrups can be supported on 'bar chairs' or hung with wire from a beam. The bar chairs are placed at a maximum distance of 600 mm apart.

THE CONCRETE MIX

A mix suitable for wall footings uses cement, concreting ('sharp') sand, coarse (20 mm) aggregate and clean water. The proportions (by volume) should be one part cement, two and a half parts sand and three and a half

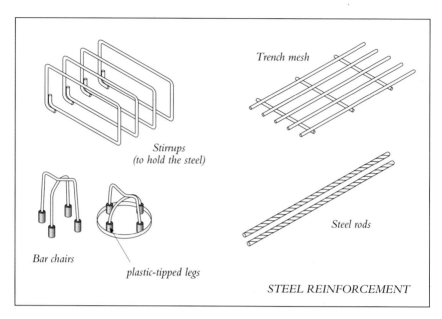

Stirrups
(to hold the steel)

Trench mesh

Steel rods

Bar chairs

plastic-tipped legs

STEEL REINFORCEMENT

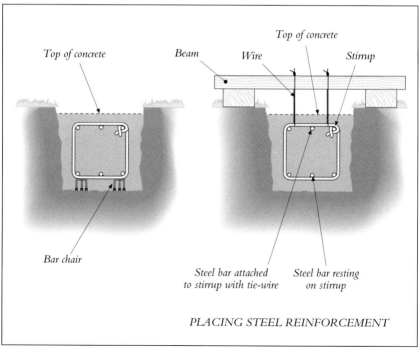

Top of concrete

Beam

Wire

Top of concrete

Stirrup

Bar chair

Steel bar attached
to stirrup with tie-wire

Steel bar resting
on stirrup

PLACING STEEL REINFORCEMENT

ORDERING FOR CONCRETE

MATERIAL	PROPORTION	QUANTITY TO FILL 1 M³
Cement	1	5.6 bags
Sand	$2^1/_2$	620 kg
20 mm aggregate	$3^1/_2$	1165 kg

parts 20 mm aggregate (1:2^1/$_2$:3^1/$_2$), and enough water to get it to a workable state. (See table above for quantities.) The concrete should hold its shape without slumping (too wet) or crumbling (too dry).

MIXING BY HAND

Concrete can be mixed by hand using a shovel, especially if only small quantities are required. Prepare the mix in a metal wheelbarrow that can be easily cleaned or on a flat surface that can be hosed down.

1 Mix the cement, sand and coarse aggregate together thoroughly while they are still dry.

2 If you are working on a flat surface, make a well in the centre of the dry mix. Add water and combine until the mix is an even colour and texture.

USING A CONCRETE MIXER

You can also mix concrete in a concrete mixer (they are available for hire). Make sure the mixer is level and on a stable surface.

1 Start by measuring out the amounts of cement, sand and 20 mm

aggregate needed. Note that the proportions are by volume. A typical hired concrete mixer produces around 85 litres of concrete – enough to lay around 1.6 m of footing for a single-thickness wall (1 m for double thickness).

2 Add half the aggregate for one mix to the drum plus some water and, with the drum revolving, add half the cement and sand in small batches.

3 Add the remaining sand, cement and aggregate (with more water as necessary) and continue to mix until the concrete is falling cleanly off the blades. Tip into a wheelbarrow. Clean the mixer immediately – or leave it running with just aggregate and water for the next batch.

READY-MIXED CONCRETE

For large amounts of concrete (for example for the base of a driveway), you can order ready-mixed concrete to be delivered by a truck. Check with local suppliers what their minimum orders are and specify what the concrete is to be used for. Make sure it has a high workability, which gives you longer to work with it before it sets hard. Finally, ensure you have several wheelbarrows available and workers to carry and spread the concrete.

LAYING THE FOOTINGS

Prepare any formwork the day before and start work early in the morning so the concrete will have time to set and can be finished before dark. Step the footings if necessary (see the diagram below). Have all the equipment ready – wheelbarrows, shovels, gum boots, timber lengths to level the concrete as you go, and floats to finish it.

1 Start at the lowest point on the site when laying the concrete, using a shovel or spade to spread it within the formwork. Keep the concrete level, checking it regularly. Make sure the concrete is packed under any steel reinforcement so it doesn't drop. If the stirrups are suspended with tie-wire from a beam, cut the tie-wire with the shovel as you work.

2 Finish the concrete 150 or 225 mm below ground level. (It is difficult to finish it precisely level and if you need to cut bricks in the lowest course they will not then be visible.) Level the concrete roughly with a shovel and then use a wooden or steel float to provide a smooth finish. A steel float gives a smoother finish than a wooden one.

3 The concrete footings must be left to cure for at least two days before you start laying the brickwork or the concrete may crack.

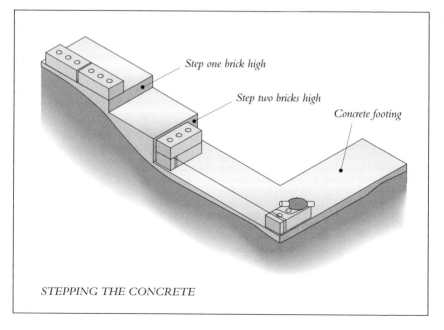

Step one brick high

Step two bricks high

Concrete footing

STEPPING THE CONCRETE

BRICK DRIVEWAYS

Driveways of brick or clay pavers are laid in essentially the same way as other forms of brick paving; however, because they will have to bear the weight of cars and other vehicles, driveways will need a substantial base.

Most driveways can be laid with a base of 100 mm of compacted hardcore and 50 mm of bedding sand, but it is very important that the hardcore is well compacted.

For a heavy duty driveway use a base of 100 mm of foundation concrete – a mix of one part cement, two and a half parts sand and three and a half parts 20 mm aggregate ($1:2^1/2:3^1/2$). When it has set, cover it with 50 mm of sand and then lay the pavers.

Edge restraints of concrete are essential for any driveway. If edges are not built, the weight of the vehicles will push out the pavers around the edge.

Hardcore and sand are an adequate base for most paved driveways.

Mortars and joints

The secret of laying bricks lies in keeping the mortar at the right consistency. The mortar joints are an integral part of a brick wall, holding the bricks in place and levelling the courses when the bricks are uneven sizes.

TOOLS AND MATERIALS

- Sand, cement and lime, or pre-mixed mortar
- Plasticiser and oxides (optional)
- Plywood mortar board or concrete mixer for mixing mortar
- Shovel
- Measure for oxides (optional)
- Trowel
- Jointer or raking tool

CONSISTENCY

Most amateur bricklayers use mortar that is too dry. To lay bricks you need mortar that is soft and pliable, a bit like toothpaste. Mortar that is too hard is very difficult to spread and joints will be uneven. It is likely to fall off the brick in a lump. Mortar that is too wet will run all over the face of the brickwork.

Mortar is useful for only about one and a half hours (a little water can be added to keep it soft and workable). After that time it loses plasticity and should be thrown out.

MATERIALS

Mortar is made from sand, cement, lime and water.

- Sand is the main ingredient in mortar, and the best sand to use is bricklayer's sand, also known as soft sand. This is finer than the 'sharp' sand used for making concrete.
- Portland or masonry cement is used for bricklaying. Cement should always be kept dry. If wet it becomes lumpy or goes hard and is unusable. Store it in a garage or shed.
- Hydrated lime (or a plasticiser) is used with Portland cement mortar to make it more workable and retard its setting time. It is purchased in bags and should also be kept dry.
- Always use clean and fresh water.

Mortars made with masonry cement or Portland cement with plasticiser are more resistant to frost damage during construction, whilst cement:lime mortars ('gauged' mortars) are more adhesive and more resistant to water penetration.

MORTAR MIXES

For normal bricklaying, use a mortar mix of one part Portland cement, one part lime and six parts sand (1:1:6) or one part masonry cement to five parts sand (1:5) with all parts by volume. Sills, copings, retaining walls and garden walls exposed to wind need stronger mixes (1:^{1}/4:4

Dry pressed bricks in the sandstock range are combined here with off-white mortar to achieve a traditional look. The joints are raked for a neat finish.

with Portland cement or 1:3 for masonry cement). See page 26 for details. For small quantities, use dry ready-mixed bricklaying mortar, sold in bags, to which you add water.

ORDERING MATERIALS FOR MORTAR

The amounts of each material you need depend on the mortar mix. For normal bricklaying, using a 1:1:6 (cement:lime:sand) mix, a 50 kg bag of Portland cement plus 50 kg lime and 330 kg of sand will be enough to lay around 500 bricks. For dry ready-mixed mortar, a 40 kg bag should lay 50 bricks.

MORTAR COLOURS

Oxides can be used to colour mortars. They come in basic colours: yellow, brown, red and black. The amount of oxide added depends on the depth of colour required. Always use a measuring gauge (a jam jar or bottle with the required level marked on it) so the colour remains the same from batch to batch. To check the colour, place the mortar on the back of a brick and leave it in the sun to dry.

For details on achieving specific colours, see the box on page 13.

MORTAR BOARDS

When the mortar has been mixed, transfer it to a mortar board, which makes it easier to pick up the mortar with a trowel.

Mortar boards are usually about 1 m² and are made from a sheet of waterproof plywood.

MORTAR MIXES (PROPORTIONS BY VOLUME)

PURPOSE	CEMENT	LIME	SAND
Normal (Portland cement)	1	1	6
Normal (masonry cement)	1	–	5
Strong (Portland cement)	1	$\frac{1}{4}$	4
Strong (Portland cement)	1	–	3

WORKING THE MORTAR

To ensure the mortar is soft and pliable, work it continuously on the board, using the trowel or, if it gets really hard, a shovel. Ideally, an assistant makes it while you lay bricks.

1 Use a smooth movement to lift the mortar off the board with a trowel.

2 Throw the mortar back on to the board and then move it to the left, softening it with the tip and edge of the trowel, and then work it back to the right in the same way.

3 Using the back of the trowel, move the mortar back across the board to finish the mixing.

MORTAR JOINTS

The mortar joints between bricks need to be finished off (pointed) whilst the mortar is still workable. There are various joint profiles.

• Flush joint. Suitable for rustic bricks or to give a smooth even surface. Create by removing the excess mortar with a trowel and rubbing the dry joint with sacking.

• Round ironed joint. Also known as a concave or 'bucket handle' joint, this is particularly suitable for use with second-hand bricks. It is created by running a round iron jointer (or a length of tubing) along the joint.

• Raked joint. Made by raking out the mortar with a piece of metal or wood (or a special tool). This joint

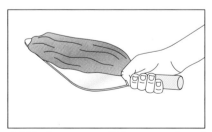

1 Lift the mortar off the mortar board with the trowel, using a wrist, elbow and shoulder movement.

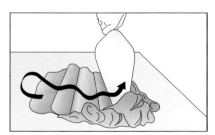

2 Begin softening the mortar by moving it to the left, using the tip and edge of the trowel.

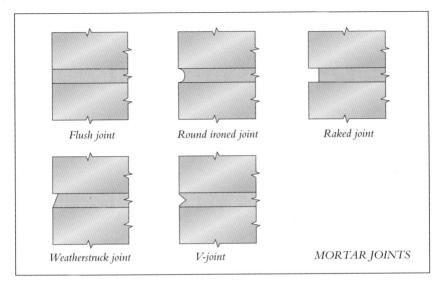

Flush joint Round ironed joint Raked joint

Weatherstruck joint V-joint *MORTAR JOINTS*

does not shed water so should only be used inside or outside with special quality bricks.

• Weatherstruck joints. Very popular for use on houses, this joint is created by shaping the mortar with a pointing trowel. It sheds water well to help rain run off the brickwork.

• V-joint. Made with a shaped jointing tool, this attractive joint also sheds water well.

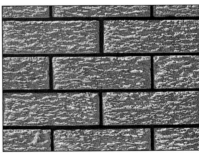

Mortar that matches the colour of the bricks gives a modern effect.

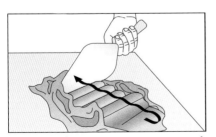

2 Using the same movement, work the mortar back towards the right, thus improving the even consistency.

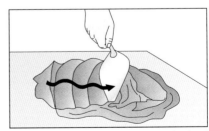

3 Turn the trowel and use the back of it to move the mortar across the board to finish the thorough mixing.

Laying bricks

Trowelling techniques and the methods used to build up a wall are the basic skills needed for bricklaying.

SETTING OUT THE BRICKWORK

Before you start laying bricks, set out the first course of bricks in a dry run to make sure the bonding in the wall is correct. Don't use mortar but allow for 10 mm vertical joints. Work from one corner only so that

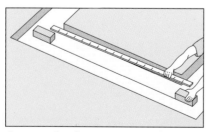

Set out the first course to check the bonding and establish the corners, or use a gauging stick as here.

you don't end up with incorrect bonding in the centre of the wall. When building a structure such as a raised bed, set out two complete sides from a corner (the other two sides will be the same).

It is worth making a gauging stick – a length of timber marked with brick lengths and widths on one side and brick thicknesses on the other (all including mortar joints), so that you can work out how many bricks will be needed along the wall and also check course heights.

TROWELLING TECHNIQUES

1 Mix up a batch of mortar, place some on the mortar board and work it to a pliable consistency (see the steps illustrated on pages 26–7). Move the mortar to the rear right-hand corner of the board (the rear left-hand corner for left handers).

2 Pick up the trowel but do not grip it too tightly. Work some mortar into the shape of the trowel and lift it off the board by sliding the trowel under it. Pick up only enough mortar to lay two or three bricks.

3 Spread the mortar on the bricks already laid (or the foundations for the first course). It takes practice to

Keeping the courses level and the walls vertical as you build are essential elements in bricklaying. String lines, held in place with corner blocks, help to keep the courses level.

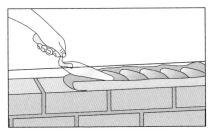

3 Spread the mortar to make a bed, holding the trowel parallel to the wall and forming a series of ridges.

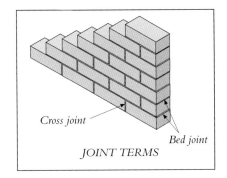

Cross joint

Bed joint

JOINT TERMS

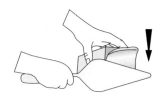

1 Scrape mortar on to end of brick.

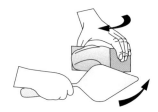

2 Spread firmly over end.

3 Remove excess mortar.

BUTTERING A BRICK TO
PUT ON A CROSS JOINT

LEVEL AND PLUMB

A spirit level is an essential tool for the bricklayer and is used to check that each course is level. It can also be used to check for plumb (vertical) and alignment, but any straight piece of timber can be used for this. If bricks are out of alignment, use your trowel handle to tap them back into place before the mortar dries.

develop the technique of ridging the mortar with the trowel but if the mortar is workable it will be easier. Hold the trowel parallel to the wall when spreading the mortar bed and move it along the wall at the same time. Spread the mortar at an even thickness of about 15–20 mm.

4 To make a cross joint, hold the brick in one hand with the end pointing forwards. Pick up enough mortar with the trowel to cover ('butter') the end of the brick with mortar, spreading it firmly over the end and removing any excess (see the drawings on the left).

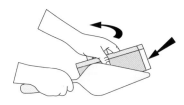

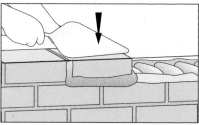

5 Place the brick on the wall, butting it first against the last brick and then pressing down on to the bed.

6 Use the trowel to tap the brick into place so that it aligns perfectly. Keep the bed joint an even thickness.

Bed and cross joints of consistent thickness make for neat brickwork.

5 Place the brick on the wall, butting it firmly against the last brick laid and then pressing it down on the laid bed of mortar.

6 Use the trowel to tap the brick into place so that it aligns perfectly and the bed joint is a consistent thickness of about 10 mm.

7 Remove the excess mortar from the bed joint by sliding the trowel along the joint, moving it upwards.

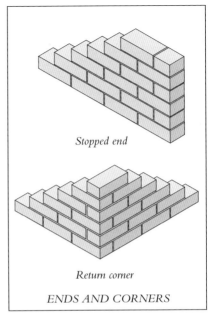

Stopped end

Return corner

ENDS AND CORNERS

8 Bring the trowel back along the bed joint and then up the cross joint to remove excess mortar.

BUILDING UP THE BRICKWORK

1 Start at the ends and corners and work inwards. Lay enough mortar on the foundations for three bricks at an end or three bricks each way at a

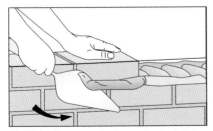

7 Slide the trowel along the bed joint to remove the excess mortar and give a neat finish.

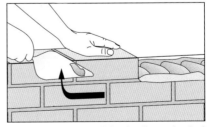

8 Bring the trowel back along the bed joint and then up the cross joint to remove excess mortar.

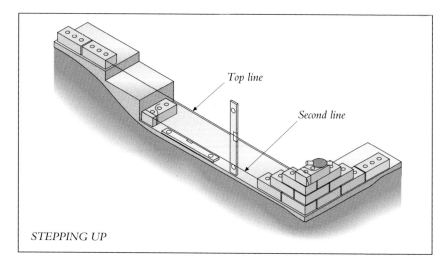

STEPPING UP

Top line

Second line

corner. Lay these bricks, check that they are level and then build up the end or corner by five courses. Follow the 'Trowelling techniques' (described on pages 28–31), checking the brick course heights with a gauging stick. Ensure each course of bricks is level, that the sides of the wall are vertical (plumb) and that any corners are square. Fit a string line between the corners or ends, using corner blocks or pins inserted into the lowest mortar course, as a guide for laying the rest of the first course.

2 Lay the first whole course of bricks between the corners (or ends), following the string line. The last (closure) brick will need to be 'buttered' at both ends to form the vertical cross mortar joints on either side of it.

3 Continue laying whole courses, keeping the mortar joints to a consistent 10 mm thickness and checking all the time for level and plumb. Move the string line up as you go and build up the corners so

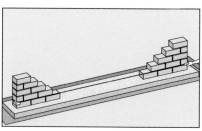

1 Use string lines fixed with pins or corner blocks to check that the courses are level and aligned.

3 When building up a corner, use a straight piece of timber to check the alignment of the courses.

octroiuntapk overst Itispvhett

that they are always higher than the rest of the brickwork. To check the alignment of the corners, use a straight piece of timber held against the wall. Tap any outstanding bricks back into place.

4 Shaped mortar joints must be finished while the mortar is wet. For weatherstruck joints and round iron jointing this is normally done after laying every second course; rake joints and V-joints are usually finished every four or six courses.

STEPPING UP
If you need to step up the brickwork, always use two level string lines. The top line runs right across the stepped gap, from the end of the built-up wall to a course above the step (see the drawing opposite). The second line is used on the lowest course so that the brickwork runs into the step evenly.

WALL JUNCTIONS
Where two walls meet in an L-junction, the brickwork of one wall must be tied in with that of the other. The tie-in ('toothing') bricks must extend into the other wall by at least one brick width.

If it is not possible to build both walls at once, holes known as 'indents' must be left in the first wall to take the tie-in bricks of the second when it is built later.

DAMP-PROOFING
Unlike house walls, which need a damp-proof course (DPC) built in to prevent damp from rising, garden walls do not need any special type of

Indent

Block indent

INDENTS

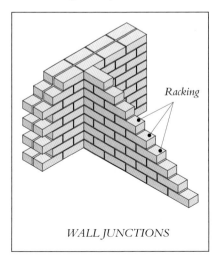

Racking

WALL JUNCTIONS

Saddle-back brick units used to provide an overlapping coping to shed rainwater. A matching coping has been used to finish the piers.

damp-proofing. Where walls are in contact with damp soil (such as retaining walls, or garden wall courses below ground), special or engineering bricks must be used and retaining walls need to have some drainage built in to them to prevent water build-up behind the wall (see page 42 for details).

What all walls need, however, is some kind of finishing at the top to prevent vertical penetration of the brickwork (which could lead to frost damage) and to throw rainwater away from the face of the wall.

The simplest method of finishing a wall is to lay bricks on edge or on end at the top of the wall (a 'soldier' course); equally simple is to add a course of shaped coping bricks or overlapping coping stones (common

on reconstituted stone walls). However, it is traditional to finish off a brick wall with a soldier course, sandwiching a 'creasing' layer of protruding clay tiles.

Brick-on-edge soldier course capping plus tile creasing.

CURVED WALLS

SETTING OUT A CIRCLE

For a complete circle, fix a stake in the centre and tie a piece of string the radius of the circle to it. Attach a metal stake to the other end and use it to draw the circle, keeping the string taut all the time. Determine the width of the foundation trench, adjust the length of the string and draw circles for either side of the trench. Set out curved walls in the same way but you may need to use a hose pipe to mark the curve.

CHOOSING BRICKS

Curved walls are most easily laid in header bond. For curves of a small radius, bricks can be cut to a tapered shape. Normal bricks may be used for curved walls and the mortar joints tapered, but only if the radius is more than 1 m or the joints will be too thick.

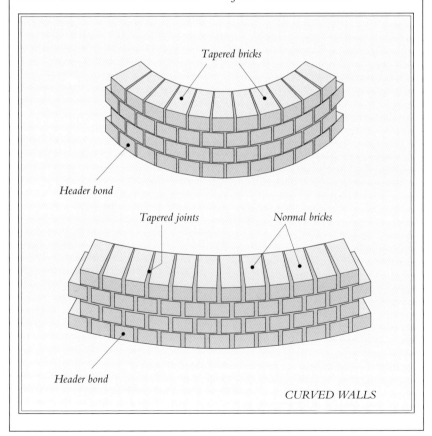

Tapered bricks

Header bond

Tapered joints

Normal bricks

Header bond

CURVED WALLS

A typical double-thickness garden wall, built in Flemish bond with intermediate piers. The wall and the piers have been finished with brick-on-edge capping and two courses of tile creasing.

Brick walls

Brick walls take many forms but the bricklaying requirements are much the same. Low garden walls are suitable projects for a home builder, as long as a few basic rules are followed.

TYPES OF BRICK WALL

There are many different types of brick wall an amateur might consider building around the home and the garden.

• Dividing walls are the most common, to form visual breaks between patio and lawn, for example, or to define the edges of pathways. Often low, dividing walls are usually a single brick thickness.

• Boundary walls surround the garden and provide both privacy and security. Normally double thickness, a boundary wall can be built up to 1.8 m high. For walls higher than 2 m, local council permission and professional structural advice will be needed.

• Retaining walls are used to create terraces in sloping gardens and also to hold back raised flowerbeds. See page 40 for more details.

• Brick and block walls are used for many garden features such as barbecues (see page 48) or planters (see page 46). Some can be treated like dividing walls, others like retaining walls.

• Screen walls neatly divide off a section of the garden without completely obscuring what is behind. They are built with pierced screen

walling blocks and pilaster piers – see pages 52–5 for further details.

DESIGNING A BRICK WALL

The way a brick wall is built depends on its height and purpose – retaining walls, in particular, need careful design (see page 40).

A single-thickness brick wall up to 450 mm high is well within the capabilities of an amateur. It may not even need a concrete foundation (if there is a solid paved area to build on) and does not need supporting piers.

All other walls will need a proper foundation as described on page 17. Single thickness walls up to 675 mm and double thickness walls higher than 1.35 m will need supporting piers at the ends and at intervals of 3 m for long walls.

Piers should be twice the thickness of the wall and can be centred on the wall or project to one side. They should be bonded to the

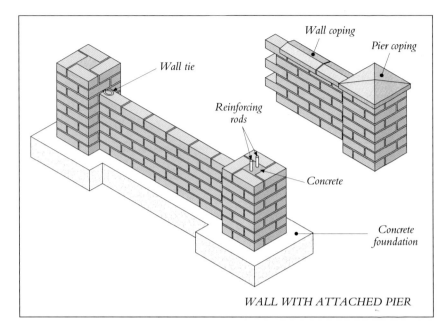

Wall coping

Pier coping

Wall tie

Reinforcing rods

Concrete

Concrete foundation

WALL WITH ATTACHED PIER

brickwork of the wall or secured to it using wall ties in each mortar course. A hollow pier will be stronger if you fill the void with concrete containing metal reinforcing rods anchored in the foundations. Remember to allow enough extra bricks to build the piers.

CAPPINGS AND COPINGS
Use a capping or coping on top of the wall to stop rainwater penetrating the brickwork. Brick cappings are the most convenient and they can be laid on edge or as a header course.

DAMP-PROOFING
A damp-proof course weakens the structure of a garden wall. Use special quality or engineering bricks for the courses below ground level. This will give adequate protection.

EXPANSION JOINTS
In long walls, include open expansion joints at a maximum of 12 m apart (usually where a panel meets a pier) to prevent cracking. Fill the gap with expansion joint filler.

FOOTINGS
Use foundation mix concrete to provide structural strength. The

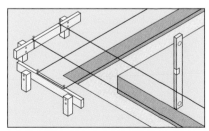

1 Set out the site with timber profiles and string lines and dig the foundation trenches.

recommended width of a concrete footing (foundation) is usually twice the width of the brick wall; the depth of the footing will depend on the height of the wall, the weight it is going to carry and the type of soil. See page 17 for further information on footings.

BUILDING A BRICK WALL

1 Calculate the number of bricks required (see the box on page 13). Set out the site with timber profiles and string lines to indicate the outlines of footing and wall. Allow for piers if necessary. Check the lines for level and dig foundation trenches (see pages 14–17).

2 Mix and pour the concrete footings, inserting reinforcement if required (see pages 18–22).

3 Move string lines to the width of the brickwork; check for level. Set out the first course dry to check the bonding and establish the corners, or use a gauging stick. Work out the bonding for any piers.

4 Lay the bricks (see pages 28–34). Build up the corners first, using water-resistant bricks for the first three courses (certainly for all courses below ground level). Check the courses are vertical with a spirit level.

5 Complete the bricklaying, checking for level and plumb with a spirit level – using a timber straight-edge to check brick alignment.

6 Add capping or coping to stop water penetration. Clean excess mortar from the bricks (see page 44).

Black expansion joint filler has been used on this wall.

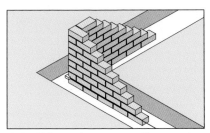

4 Build up the corners first, using water-resistant bricks for the first three courses.

5 Complete the bricklaying, checking for level and plumb (vertical). Check alignment with a batten.

Retaining walls

Retaining walls can be used for many different purposes: to make terraces on a sloping site or just to hold the soil in a garden bed. Small ones can be constructed by the home builder but high ones (1.2 m and over) should be designed by a structural engineer.

TOOLS AND MATERIALS

See boxes on pages 14, 18, 24 and 28.

- Drain pipe (optional)
- Hardcore
- Steel reinforcing bars for piers

PLANNING

When planning a strong retaining wall you need to consider a number of factors:
- how much weight is to be retained by the wall;
- the materials that will be used for building the wall;
- what sort of drainage is required.

LOAD BEHIND THE WALL

The soil load behind a retaining wall puts great pressure on it, which is why a high retaining wall should always be designed by a structural engineer or it may collapse after heavy rain. Never use clay soil for backfilling as it expands and shrinks, and the wall may crack. Use hardcore topped with sandy soil.

RETAINING WALL MATERIALS

You can use any of the normal wall building materials for creating a retaining wall.

Bricks (or reconstituted stone blocks) are the usual choice, but bricks must be water-resistant and should be laid either as a full brick thickness wall, preferably with one of the stronger bonds (English bond or Flemish bond), or as two single skins (a bit like a cavity wall) held together with wall ties, with the gap between filled with concrete or mortar and reinforced with vertical steel bars. Retaining walls more than 1 m (3 ft 3 in) high need to be reinforced with piers at least at either end. High walls may need to have three thicknesses of brick for the first few courses.

Hollow concrete blocks are another good choice as you can fill the voids with concrete (and reinforcing bars) – but you will want to paint the exposed surface or to cover it with some kind of render.

Natural stone is also a good choice for a retaining wall (since it is heavy), but the wall will need to be much thicker at the bottom and laid to a 'batter' – that is, leaning slightly backwards into the slope.

All retaining walls should be built with full concrete foundations and a 'strong' mortar mix should always be used (see page 26).

A steep slope has been terraced and a series of retaining walls built to support wide garden beds. The high wall was professionally designed to withstand the pressure of the soil and rainwater behind it.

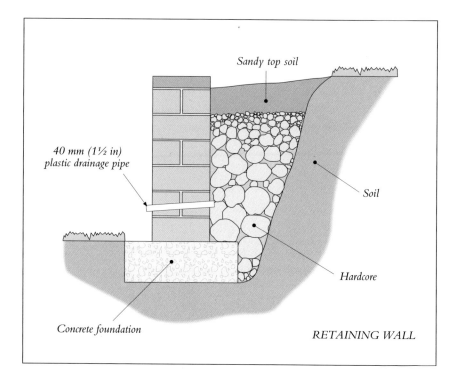

Sandy top soil

40 mm (1½ in)
plastic drainage pipe

Soil

Hardcore

Concrete foundation

RETAINING WALL

DRAINAGE

Water will collect behind a retaining wall and you must provide some way for it to be removed. The simplest method is to leave 'weep' holes by not putting mortar in some of the vertical joints low down in the wall; alternatively, you can install 40 mm plastic drainage pipes passing through the wall from the backfilling material.

If a large amount of water comes through the wall, you may need to install a surface drain on the ground below the wall to take it away.

ATTACHED PIERS

If a very strong wall is required, add attached piers (usually one and a half or two bricks square) at the back. Filled with concrete or mortar, they are reinforced with vertical steel bars.

BUILDING A RETAINING WALL

1 Calculate the number of bricks required (see page 13), allowing for piers. Remove enough soil from the site to lay the foundations and to build the wall – if necessary, hold the soil back with heavy timber boards. Set out timber profiles for the footing and wall positions, including piers, and excavate the trench for the footings (see pages 14–17).

2 Place steel reinforcement in the trench if required and pour in the

concrete. A retaining wall should be centred on its concrete footings. Anchor bars vertically for the piers and ensure the top of the footings is level (see pages 18–22).

3 Lay the bricks (see pages 28–34), leaving weep holes every third vertical (cross) joint in the first full course of bricks above ground level or installing regular drainage pipes through the wall, chipping the corners off bricks as necessary to fit.

4 Backfill behind the wall with hardcore (stones and broken bricks), with the largest pieces at the bottom, and finish off with light sandy soil.

5 Clean the brickwork (see page 44).

Retaining walls have been used here to hold back the garden and to create a patio area with raised flowerbeds.

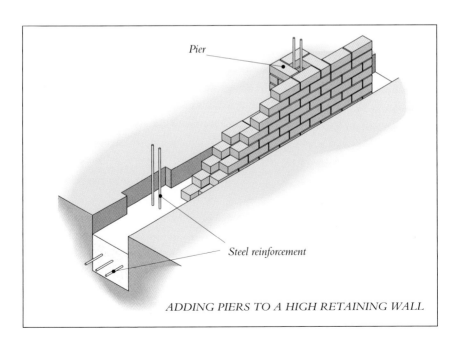

ADDING PIERS TO A HIGH RETAINING WALL

Pier

Steel reinforcement

Curved walls

A curved wall makes a stylish garden feature whether it is freestanding or used for a small structure such as the raised planter shown opposite.

TOOLS AND MATERIALS

See boxes on pages 14, 18, 24 and 28.

CIRCULAR PLANTER

1 Choose the bricks and assemble your materials and tools. Facing bricks are suitable for a planter as they do not absorb water. Use a strong mortar mix of one part cement, one quarter part lime and four parts sand (1:^{1}/$_4$:4).

2 Lay out the circular shape (see the box on page 35). Dig out the trench.

3 Lay the concrete foundations (see pages 18–22). Steel reinforcement is not necessary for a low wall. In fact, if the wall is only a few courses high, a 50 mm layer of sand or existing paving may be sufficient foundation.

4 Set out the entire first course of bricks, allowing for the tapered joints, and adjust the joints as necessary. Circular shapes are best laid entirely in header bond.

5 Lay the bricks (see pages 28–34), checking for level and plumb. Add a capping to stop water penetration.

6 Clean the bricks (see below).

CLEANING BRICKS

Let the brickwork dry for three days and clean off all excess mortar. Bricks are best cleaned with a solution of hydrochloric acid and water, one part acid to twenty parts water. Always add the acid to the water so the acid will be less likely to splash you.

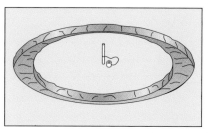

2 Set out the circular shape using a string from a central stake, then dig out the foundation trench.

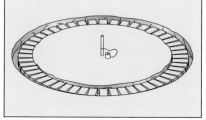

4 Set out the entire first course, allowing for the tapered joints, and adjust the joints as necessary.

Curved walls are best laid in header bond, and in this large planter the top course was laid on edge to produce a neat capping course. Facing bricks were used for the project and the joints tapered to produce the curve.

Concrete walling blocks

Reconstituted stone concrete walling blocks make a change from clay bricks. They introduce an additional range of pleasing effects and can sometimes be easier to lay.

TOOLS AND MATERIALS

See boxes on pages 14, 18, 24 and 28.

● Reconstituted stone blocks

● Matching capping stones

● Walling adhesive and spreader (optional)

PLANNING

Concrete walling blocks come in a range of styles and finishes, many to imitate genuine stone walling. Some are brick-sized; others are larger. Blocks have one, two or three finished faces and also come in two-thirds lengths (to avoid cutting). Most ranges of concrete walling have their own matching capping in sizes to suit the main walling.

Concrete blocks can be laid in mortar (1:1:5 for Portland cement: lime:sand or 1:4 for masonry cement: sand) in exactly the same way as bricks – the alternative with some types of concrete block is to use walling adhesive which you apply with a spreader.

BUILDING A CONCRETE BLOCK WALL

A concrete block wall is set out in exactly the same way as a brick wall. High or thick walls will need proper concrete foundations (see pages 18–22), but low single-thickness walls can be built on a compacted bed of sand or on existing paving (a paving slab patio, for example).

Check the manufacturer's literature for the number of blocks required for each square metre of walling – note the adhesive gives only a 3 mm gap between blocks. If foundations are required, set out the

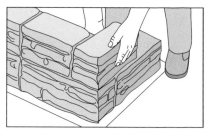

Walling adhesive is applied with a spreader to the foundations or on the blocks already laid.

Large concrete walling blocks make laying quicker. This two-thirds block is being used to finish a corner.

site with timber profiles and string lines and dig out trenches before mixing and pouring the concrete for the foundations (see pages 14–22).

With mortar, set out and lay the blocks as for bricks (pages 28–34). Alternatively, spread a layer of walling adhesive on the foundation or the blocks already laid. Complete the blocklaying, checking for level and plumb (large blocks make laying quicker). Add matching capping stones, using more mortar or walling adhesive. Leave to set.

Reconstituted stone blocks, complete with their own capping, have been used for the retaining wall holding the rear boundary wall and the flowerbed, which is on two different levels.

Barbecue

A brick or concrete block barbecue is an excellent beginner's project and makes an attractive and useful addition to the garden. Add provision for fuel storage and surfaces for serving food.

TOOLS AND MATERIALS
See boxes on pages 14, 18, 24 and 28.

• Concrete walling blocks
• Barbecue kit
• Paving slab and coping stones
• Expanding wallbolts (6)
• Electric drill and masonry bit
• Spanner
• Walling adhesive and spreader (optional)

PLANNING
When planning a barbecue, you need to consider the following.
• Size – how many people will it have to cook for?
• The fuel to be used – charcoal in a tray is the normal choice, but you should be able to adapt this design to suit a bottled gas barbecue.
• The location – choose a level site, sheltered from the wind, with access to the kitchen. Avoid fire hazards such as overhanging branches and timber fencing and think about the effects on your neighbours.

FOUNDATIONS
A barbecue is a light structure and, except on very soft soil, a 50 mm layer of compacted sand or existing paving such as a patio should be sufficient.

If you do lay foundations, use a foundation mix concrete (see pages 18–22 for details).

MATERIALS
A barbecue can be built from well-burnt bricks (not calcium silicate) which will be able to withstand the heat from the barbecue.

This project uses concrete walling blocks, which come in two sizes (standard and two-thirds lengths). The normal blocks have just one finished face; 'quoin end' blocks have a finished end as well and are used for exposed ends and corners; all other faces are flat and smooth.

A barbecue 'kit' consists of a cooking grill and a tray for holding the charcoal and it can be secured to the walls with wallbolts held in holes drilled into the walls or inserted in the mortar courses.

A storage area is incorporated under the charcoal tray and the top of the barbecue is finished off with coping stones. A paving slab provides a seat or serving area.

If mortar is used for constructing the barbecue it should be a fairly weak mix (1:1:6 cement:lime:sand) which will allow a little movement as the blocks heat up and cool down.

A patio next to the house is an ideal site for building a permanent brick or block barbecue. The patio paving will provide sufficient foundation.

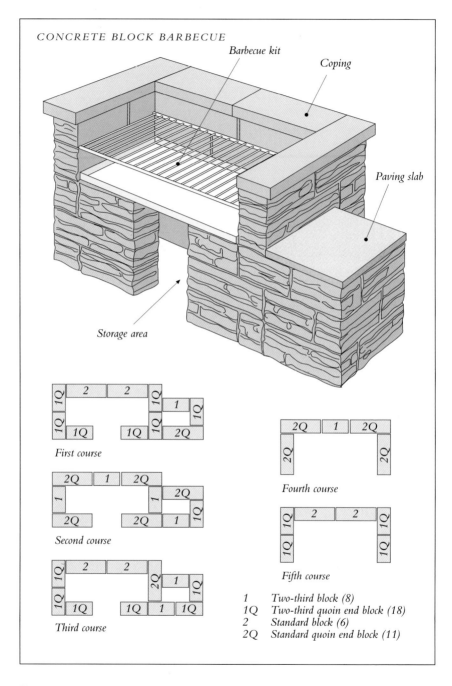

CONCRETE BLOCK BARBECUE

Barbecue kit

Coping

Paving slab

Storage area

First course

Second course

Third course

Fourth course

Fifth course

1   Two-third block (8)
1Q   Two-third quoin end block (18)
2   Standard block (6)
2Q   Standard quoin end block (11)

BUILDING THE BARBECUE

1 You do not need to lay concrete foundations for a simple barbecue. Existing paving should be perfectly satisfactory or use a 50 mm layer of well-compacted sand. Make sure, however, that the surface is level.

2 Lay the blocks dry on the surface, fitted around the barbecue kit. Mark the surface for the first course, taking the marked lines beyond the blocks, and spread a bed of mortar or a layer of walling adhesive.

3 Starting at one corner, lay a 'quoin end' block, adjusting it until it is aligned with the marks, and then lay the next block up against it, with more mortar or adhesive in between.

4 Continue building up three courses, using more mortar or adhesive, following the diagrams opposite. Use a spirit level to ensure that each course is horizontal and that the walls are vertical.

5 Once the fourth and fifth courses have been built on the main structure the basic barbecue is complete. If using mortar, the supporting bolts for the charcoal tray and cooking grill can be built into the mortar joints below the fourth and fifth courses.

6 Lay the single 450 mm square paving slab on the hollow seat (again using mortar or adhesive – unless you want it to be removable for an additional storage area) and fit the copings to the top of the fifth course of blocks. The coping blocks will need to be cut down to size to allow a 12 mm overhang for the side pieces and to fit the two pieces at the back. Cut them by first making a groove around the cutting line with a club hammer and cold chisel and then giving the line a gentle tap with the same tools.

7 If you have used adhesive, drill holes in the walls to fit the wallbolts – two at each side for the cooking grill and two at the back for the charcoal tray (which sits on blocks at the front). Put in the bolts, using a spanner, and put the grill and charcoal tray in place.

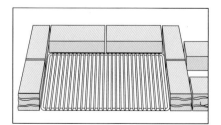

2 Lay the first course of blocks out dry around the barbecue kit to make sure they are correctly positioned.

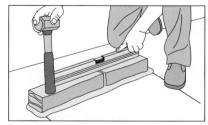

3 Start at a corner laying a quoin end block to the marked lines. Lay the next block and check levels.

Screen block walling

A screen block wall can be used in lots of different ways in the garden – and has the advantage that it will allow both light and air to pass through it. It is easy to build.

USES

A screen block wall is normally used to divide one part of a garden from another where you do not want total exclusion. It is ideal around a patio to provide privacy and shelter without a significant loss of light and air. It can also be used effectively to 'hide' parts of the garden you do not want to be seen – such as a composting area.

MATERIALS

• Pierced screen blocks are made from concrete and usually coloured white or off white. They are 290 mm square and 90 mm thick and are about 50 per cent air, which allows light through (matching patterned solid blocks are also available). Screen blocks can be used on their own or incorporated in walling with reconstituted stone blocks.

• Unusually, for walling, pierced screen walling blocks are laid in stack bond (one on top of another); the wall is normally given strength by pilaster blocks, built as piers, which have a locating groove in one or more sides to support the screen blocks. Pilasters with one groove are used at the ends of walls, while corner pilasters and intermediate pilasters (fitted every 3 m) have two grooves.

• Each pilaster block is 190 mm high, so three blocks (plus two 10 mm mortar courses) is equal to two screen blocks (plus one 10 mm mortar course). The pilasters are hollow, and can be filled with mortar and reinforced with steel rods set into the foundation concrete.

• Matching 600 mm copings are made for the walling blocks and decorative caps for the pilaster piers. Coping stones help to hold the wall together as well as protecting it and improving its appearance.

• Screen block walling can be built using mortar as for brick walls (except that you should use white Portland cement and sand), but you can also use walling adhesive – more appropriate when using them with reconstituted stone walling blocks.

Pierced screen blocks often make effective dividing or boundary walls. They allow air and light through so are good for plants.

PLANNING

Low screen block walls (up to 1 m) can be built directly on existing paving, but higher walls will need a proper concrete foundation.

Additional strength is provided by reinforcing rods inside the pilasters and also by wire mesh laid where the wall bed joints coincide with the pilaster bed joints.

When planning the length and height of the wall, remember that you must work in units of 300 mm – and it will be better with lengths in multiples of 600 mm, so that you do not have to cut coping stones to fit.

BUILDING A SCREEN BLOCK WALL

1 Calculate the number of blocks required – eleven for each square metre of walling, but remember that the wall must be designed in units of 300 mm or, preferably, 600 mm.

2 Set out the site with timber profiles and string lines to indicate the outlines of the footings and the wall and the position of the pilaster piers.

Check the lines for level and dig trenches (see pages 14–17).

3 Mix and pour the concrete footings (see pages 18–22), inserting steel reinforcement starter bars at the positions of the pilaster piers. Extend these bars once the concrete has set by wiring on reinforcing rods.

4 Move the string lines to the width of the pilaster piers and set pilaster and walling blocks out dry (with spacers to simulate the 10 mm mortar gaps) to check the spacing. The piers should not be more than 3 m (ten blocks) apart.

5 Mortar the first pilaster pier in place around a starter bar and reinforcing rod (see pages 28–34 for trowelling techniques), taking it up two blocks. Position the first two blocks of the second pier without mortar and set a string line over the top of the two piers to act as a guide when laying the walling blocks.

6 Spread mortar on the foundations sufficient for two blocks. Dampen

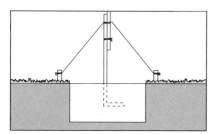

3 When laying the foundations, incorporate an L-shaped steel starter bar for the pier reinforcing rods.

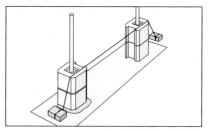

5 With the first two pilaster blocks mortared into place, set up the other pier dry and lay a string line.

the blocks with water first (in order to prevent the mortar drying out too quickly) and lay them on the mortar bed, buttering one side of each block with mortar. The first block must be fitted firmly into the locating groove in the pilaster pier. Continue laying the first course of blocks, using a spirit level to make sure it is level.

7 When you get to the position of the second pier, mortar the first block of this in place as well – and continue the first course to further piers if the wall is longer than 3 m or goes round a corner. Then lay the second course of walling blocks (this time slotting both end blocks into their piers).

8 After the second course of walling blocks, add the third pilaster block (which should be level) and lay some metal reinforcing mesh in the next mortar bed over the top of the walling blocks taking it into the pier. Add another pilaster block and fill the centre of the pilaster piers with mortar. Continue laying pilaster

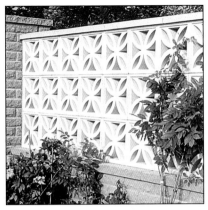

Screen block walling (here used without pilasters) can be very effectively incorporated into a reconstituted stone block wall.

blocks and screen walling blocks until the wall is the finished height, using more mesh reinforcing strip every other walling course.

9 Finish off by adding the coping stones on top of the walling blocks, mortaring these in place, and adding caps to the pilaster piers. Clean all loose mortar off the face of the walling blocks and pilaster piers and give the mortar in the joints a neat recessed or flush finish.

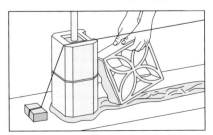

6 The first screen block needs to be buttered with mortar on one side and is inserted into the pilaster groove.

8 Add metal reinforcement mesh to every other screen mortar course and fill the pilaster piers with mortar.

Bricking up openings

Bricking up an unwanted opening – a doorway or window – is a fiddly job and to get a good result you need to lay the bricks correctly and match the materials.

METHOD

1 Select bricks and mortar to match the existing ones (see box, page 13). Match bricks for colour, texture and size. Remove the timber frames and wedges from the openings, taking care not to damage the brickwork.

2 Remove any half bricks from the edges of the opening so that the bonding will continue unbroken. Clean all mortar from the brickwork in the opening. Work slowly so as not to damage brick corners or crack

the bricks. Hard mortar joints may need to be drilled out or cleaned out with a plugging chisel.

3 Set out the first course to make sure the new courses will align exactly with the old ones. You may need to cut the bricks for the first course so that they will fit properly and allow the upper courses to align.

4 Thoroughly wet the old brickwork so the new mortar will bond to it with maximum strength.

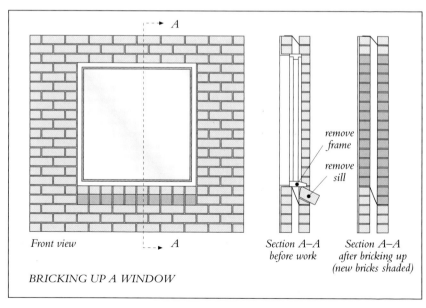

A

remove frame

remove sill

Front view   *A*

Section A–A before work

Section A–A after bricking up (new bricks shaded)

BRICKING UP A WINDOW

5 Lay the bricks, using a string line or straight-edge to keep each course level. Completely fill the bed joints and cross joints with mortar. Take care to keep the bricks level and plumb and aligned with the courses in the existing wall. Make a visual check after each course.

6 When laying the last course of bricks, add enough mortar to the top of the bricks to fill the joint completely so that the new brickwork is bonded as strongly as possible to the existing work.

7 Clean off all excess mortar from the bricks before they dry. The bricks can be cleaned with hydrochloric acid and water (20 parts water to 1 part acid) three days after you have finished the bricklaying.

The doorway above this stone threshold has been partly bricked up and a window inserted. A neater result could have been obtained by using cut bricks for the first course instead of bricks laid on edge. The bricks could not be matched exactly and so the wall has been painted.

Repairing brickwork

Crumbling mortar and broken bricks can be replaced, and cracks repaired, without damaging the rest of the wall.

REPOINTING AND REPLACING BRICKS

One of the most common problems of brick walls is crumbling mortar. If you see deteriorating joints, you can replace the mortar to prevent major faults developing. Broken bricks are removed and replaced the same way.

1 Use a plugging chisel and a club hammer to remove any mortar that is loose or around broken bricks. Remove the bed joint first, then the top joint and then the two cross joints. Remove the brick.

2 Clean the cavity. Use a paint brush to dampen the bricks to prevent the mortar drying out too quickly.

3 Mix up mortar to a suitable colour and consistency. Replace the mortar on the bed joint first, then the cross joints and then apply mortar to the top of the brick. Replace the brick slowly, making sure the mortar does not fall off. Ensure any gaps in the mortar are filled. You can support the brick on a piece of plywood as you slide it in.

4 Repoint the mortar, making sure that the joints have the same profile as the existing joints.

CRACKS

Cracks appear in brickwork when the structure settles or shifts. They should be repaired before they get too large by removing the mortar to a depth of at least 5 cm (2 in) or until the mortar is solid. Then replace the mortar as described above.

Cracks that reappear may indicate a serious problem. Consult a building surveyor to determine the cause.

1 Remove all mortar, removing the bed joint first, then the top joint, then the two cross joints.

3 Mortar the bed and cross joints and the top of the brick. Replace the brick and fill any gaps.

Tools for bricklaying

Some of the most useful tools for bricklaying are shown below. Build up your tool kit gradually – most of the tools can be purchased from your local hardware store.

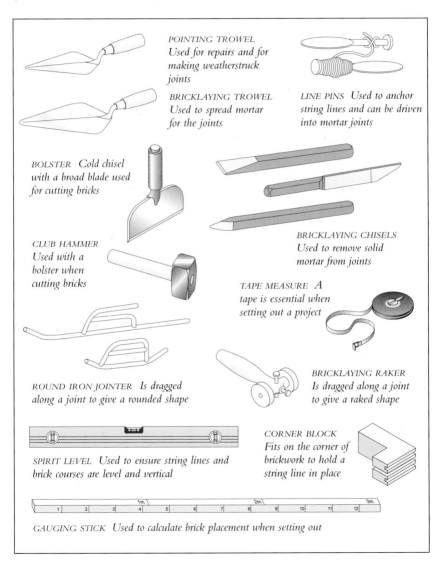

POINTING TROWEL *Used for repairs and for making weatherstruck joints*

BRICKLAYING TROWEL *Used to spread mortar for the joints*

LINE PINS *Used to anchor string lines and can be driven into mortar joints*

BOLSTER *Cold chisel with a broad blade used for cutting bricks*

CLUB HAMMER *Used with a bolster when cutting bricks*

BRICKLAYING CHISELS *Used to remove solid mortar from joints*

TAPE MEASURE *A tape is essential when setting out a project*

ROUND IRON JOINTER *Is dragged along a joint to give a rounded shape*

BRICKLAYING RAKER *Is dragged along a joint to give a raked shape*

SPIRIT LEVEL *Used to ensure string lines and brick courses are level and vertical*

CORNER BLOCK *Fits on the corner of brickwork to hold a string line in place*

GAUGING STICK *Used to calculate brick placement when setting out*

Paving

Recycled house bricks laid in a herringbone pattern form a handsome feature of this compact courtyard. A circular bed at the centre accommodates an established crepe myrtle and simple foliage plants.

Planning your paving

Carefully laid paving can transform the exterior landscape of your home into a functional yet decorative setting for a range of occasions. Consider your needs before drawing up a plan.

WHEN TO PAVE

Paving enables you to move around outside the home and create specialist areas within your landscape design. Construct these low-maintenance, hard-surface areas before adding the softer embellishments of garden beds, plants and lawns.

Paths and driveways – the 'high traffic lanes' – are the most commonly paved areas around a home, but you can use paving to define outdoor living spaces such as courtyards, patios and pool surrounds and add colour and style by introducing patterns and texture.

Paving materials are especially useful where there are changes of level or drainage problems.

BENEFITS OF PAVING

Although there are many ways of providing hard-surface areas around your home, paving offers additional benefits to the home landscaper.

• Paving provides a hard-wearing, long-term surface with an attractive finish that weathers well.

• It can be used effectively in the formation of a path, driveway or entertainment area, directing movement or providing space in which to sit and relax.

• Correctly paved areas require little maintenance in any setting.

• Paving projects can be undertaken with success by the home landscaper.

• Paving materials come in a variety of styles and colours that blend or contrast with other surfaces such as lawn, garden beds and water.

• Paved areas can be used in either formal or informal settings.

• Pavers can be laid in a variety of patterns to cater for individual tastes.

• Paving materials are available to suit any situation or budget.

PLANNING

Paved areas are an extension of your living space, so plan to incorporate natural features such as trees, gardens and exposed rock surfaces to ensure your project is in harmony with its setting rather than imposed on it.

Begin by drawing a detailed plan of your house and land. Mark the key points such as entry doors, the garage, gates and specific parts of your garden that require connection via a path. Note the places where you like to relax or entertain, or areas that are shady or constantly damp. Plan to connect the proposed hard-surface areas around your home in an interesting but practical way.

Next, consider the shape and size of your proposed paving and the impact such areas will have on the appearance of your home.

DRIVEWAYS

A driveway is a focal point; in fact, it is often the first thing a visitor notices. Constructing a driveway to blend with the architectural style of the house and its garden setting is important. A straight driveway creates a formal approach to a home, whereas a curved or sweeping driveway appears more inviting. A circular driveway, which becomes a feature when a garden, statuary or a pond is added, is an option on a wide-fronted block.

PATHS

Paved paths direct traffic and reduce the amount of dirt and mud carried in from outdoors. As well as leading visitors to the main entrance of the house, they provide protection for plants and lawn.

Straight paths give a formal and direct approach and usually lead to entrances, exits or work areas (such as a tool shed or clothes drying area). Meandering paths often blend with the garden and are designed to take the traveller on a leisurely stroll to a seat, courtyard or swimming pool.

ENTRIES

The entry to a home may incorporate a porch, a foyer, a verandah, steps or a ramp, all of which can be created with your choice of paving materials.

Beautiful, tessellated tiled patterns have been a feature of verandahs and porches for many years. More recent styles have turned to the use of natural stone, slate, terracotta, ceramic and brick for an elegant yet hardwearing finish for entry areas and steps.

RELAXATION AREAS

Areas for home relaxation include patios, terraces, courtyards, barbecue surrounds and swimming pools. As these form a transition between the house and the garden, it is vital that the material and style work in harmony with the home.

WATER FEATURES

Pools and ponds are often set slightly apart from the home, swimming pools being separated from the main body of the yard by safety fencing. Garden ponds are usually situated in a shady corner designed as a restful nook. Paving is an ideal treatment for such areas, which are usually damp. Near swimming pools, it provides a safe, non-slip surface and an attractive edge and coping material. Take special care, as the chosen material must be tolerant of either salt or chlorine and other pool chemicals.

SHADY AREAS

Paving is ideal on damp or shaded ground where grass will not grow. Brighten areas overshadowed by large trees or buildings by installing a garden seat, fountain or statue on a firm surface of patterned pavers.

MAINTAINING YOUR PAVING

DISGUISING TREE ROOT DAMAGE

Uplifting or cracking by tree roots usually occurs over many years.

• If the tree cannot be moved or pruned, introduce a curve or circle to redirect the paving around the troubled area.

• If the damage affects only part of a long length of paving, create a slight, unobtrusive undulation to disguise it and maintain the existing direction. Re-lay the pavers in the damaged section and for several metres on both sides.

CORRECTING SINKAGE

Uneven sections appear in paving due to subsidence in the base material. Lift the surface layer of pavers, bricks or stone, and correct minor sinkages by adding extra bedding sand. If the problem is significant, loosen the surface of the base material, rake in dry cement, recompact the base and replace the pavers.

CLEANING BRICK PAVING

Unsightly blemishes on paving can be removed with basic care.

• Efflorescence appears as a white, powdery discolouration on the surface of new bricks or pavers. It is the result of soluble salts being drawn to the surface by moisture. Remove efflorescence by dry brushing with a stiff-bristled brush or broom. Washing with a hose does not solve the problem, as the offending crystals are simply dissolved back into the brickwork.

• Contain growths such as moulds, lichens and mosses by ensuring unnecessary moisture does not accumulate under paved surfaces. Expose affected areas to increased sunlight – thereby allowing them to dry out – by removing or pruning back overhanging plants or trees. Use a spade or stiff-bristled brush to scrub away the bulk of the material, then treat the area with a bleach or fungicidal solution.

• Wear protective clothing when using an acid-based wash for removing stains. A mixture of 10:1 water and hydrochloric acid is appropriate, but acid can cause discolouration and damage some timbers and metals. If necessary, lift, turn over and re-lay the pavers.

CLEANING STONE AND TILES

Earthenware tiles are difficult to stain and exposure to the elements usually keeps them clean. Around barbecues or where grease or oil spills are likely to occur, sealing is the most feasible option. Maintain slate and sandstone by sweeping regularly and washing with clean water, or mix 5 litres of water with 250 millilitres of chlorine bleach for use as a scrub.

Freshly laid clay pavers introduce the warmth of terracotta to this Mediterranean-style garden and brighten what could otherwise be a rather dim corner. Earthy, hard-wearing materials are ideal in shady locations such as this.

Basic materials

Modern pavers are available in clay, concrete, slate, marble, granite, sandstone and other manufactured finishes. Paving is also possible with standard house bricks or natural flagstones.

CHOOSING MATERIALS

Once you have decided where to pave, select the most suitable material for the job.

Some of the most common paving materials are:

- clay pavers (or paving stones)
- house bricks
- concrete pavers (or paving stones)
- slate or marble
- cut or split stone (such as sandstone)
- natural flagstones
- ceramic, terracotta or concrete tiles
- imitation sandstone, limestone, slate and granite
- granite setts

Consider the architectural style of your home, the degree of formality in your setting, your budget and the availability of materials. Non-slip surfaces are essential for paving exposed to the elements or in areas prone to dampness or moss growth.

CLAY PAVERS

The greater strength and hardness of clay pavers give them an advantage over house bricks and make them ideal for heavy traffic areas such as driveways. They are also better suited for use in corrosive situations such as around salt-water swimming pools. Consistently rectangular clay pavers can be tessellated to create a choice of patterns and, because they are flat on both sides, chipped corners can be hidden on the downward face.

Clay pavers are available in a variety of sizes, 230 x 115 x 50 mm being the most useful. As this width is exactly half the length, it is possible to create interlocking designs (such as basketweave) as well as standard paving patterns. Both clay pavers and house bricks come in warm, earthy colours, and clay, being a natural material, provides a richness that does not fade over time. In exposed situations, dark clay absorbs heat, becoming very hot, particularly in the summer. Light colours stay cooler and can make an area appear larger, but in damp, shaded areas or under shedding foliage, staining and moss growth become more apparent.

HOUSE BRICKS

House bricks (both new and old) are an alternative to commercial pavers. The rustic appeal of house bricks adds an 'old-world' charm to any setting, particularly if you are able to purchase original sandstocks. They are best suited to courtyards, paths and patios, and should not be used around swimming pools.

When combining materials, identify a common theme: here, it is the russet tones of the clay and slate.

Before using house bricks in driveways, discuss their suitability with the supplier.

House bricks usually measure 230 x 110 x 76 mm, so in an interlocking pattern such as basketweave the joints are slightly wider than usual as the length-to-width ratio is not exactly 2:1. Slight variations in dimension make positioning more difficult.

With their 76 mm depth, standard bricks require deeper excavation than is necessary when laying clay pavers. Dry-pressed house bricks (or solids) have a frog in one side to assist in the bonding of the mortar bed, so each is left with only one possible exposed surface. Extruded house bricks (or wire cuts) are manufactured with holes running through their centres and must be laid on one edge, making them relatively fragile in use.

CONCRETE PAVERS

Standard pavers made from concrete – some available with spacing lugs on the sides – help make laying simple.

Modern, fade-resistant concrete pavers are often made to resemble natural products (such as sawn sandstone, slate, split granite and even terrazzo, with honed and polished surfaces). Many are manufactured as 20 mm thick tiles as well as 50 mm thick pavers.

The cobblestone has a time-worn appearance, particularly when the edges are rumbled. With its dimensions of approximately 230 x 190 x 50 mm, the cobblestone is unsuitable for some patterns (such as basketweave). Instead, choose from the range of geometric-shaped pavers, which are easier to lay in interlocking patterns.

Suitable for any paving pattern, the standard concrete paver (230 x 115 mm) is appropriate because of its 2:1 length to width ratio. For additional strength in driveways, irregular, interlocking pavers are produced in a variety of sizes and patterns. Concrete products vary in thickness. The thinner 40 mm pavers are ideal for pedestrian-only areas such as courtyards, terraces and swimming pool surrounds. For domestic driveways, a 50 mm thickness copes with normal traffic.

For heavier traffic in industrial and commercial situations, pavers of 60 mm thickness are recommended.

A concrete product known as Driveline 50 is manufactured from a mix of limestone, cement and aggregate wet-cast into moulds which vibrate mechanically to produce an extremely hard-wearing finish. The product has the texture and colour of natural stone but the strength of concrete. Available in different sizes with a 50 mm width, Driveline pavers are much larger than traditional paving blocks but do not suffer from loss of strength.

STONE
Any flat-surfaced rock is suitable for use as flagging.
• Igneous rocks (such as granite and basalt) are formed from molten magna or lave. Many of the early nineteenth-century cobbled streets were made from very hard basalt known as bluestone. Granite is a popular paving material, particularly as road inserts and in large public areas. The surface of granite is extremely hardwearing and durable but this stone is expensive.
• Sedimentary rocks (including limestone) are formed by the steady build-up of fossilized remains, seashells, sand or existing rock. Sandstone blocks (commonly 800 x 400 x 50 mm) are sold with one or both main surfaces sawn. Split sandstone is irregular in shape and is suited to a more informal setting. Although heavy, sandstone is a soft material, easy for the home paver to cut and lay. New sandstone weathers quickly, as it is porous, and it soon begins to appear aged. Sandstone's natural non-slip surface provides an excellent built-in safety element. It is a popular material for steps, courtyards, verandahs, paths and patios, and can be laid safely around chlorinated swimming pools.
• Metamorphic rocks are formed by heat or pressure resulting from movement of the earth's crust. The best-known examples are marble and slate. Marble chips are used in terrazzo floors and paving.

SLATE
Slate is created by the compression of clays, shales and volcanic ash and can be split along planes of cleavage to thicknesses of as little as 5 mm. As a metamorphic rock with low porosity, it is generally difficult to stain. The exception occurs when slate is laid around a barbecue, where it is exposed to oil and grease spills.

Most commercial slates originate in Africa, China, Britain, Belgium, Spain, India or Italy. Some specialist importers deal in the best-quality slate from Africa, which is quite expensive to buy. It comes in dark mottled tones of black, gold and red and, as darker colours absorb heat, this slate is most suited to interior or shaded areas. For open exterior paving, lighter coloured slate (such as the Chinese or Indian varieties) is recommended. Chinese slate is available in tones ranging from brown to green and is suitable for use in outdoor situations (including in and around swimming pools). Some Chinese green slate is rich in iron pyrites or 'fool's gold'.

The Indian type of slate is usually a combination of mottled brown, pink, silver and red. The Indian variety is cheaper than African slate but often contains iron oxide, making it unsuitable for use around pools and in other wet situations in which rust staining occurs. Other exotic slates are more expensive.

Slate tiles can be purchased with cut, handsawn or chipped edges. Cut-edged tiles are uniform in size and give a formal finish to paving. Handsawn slate varies slightly in dimension but has neat edges on both sides. Chipped slate is guillotined, causing breaking or chipping on one side. This means laying is usually restricted to only one surface, with the chipped side facing down.

TILES

Tiles are available in a wide price bracket and range from plain terracotta to complicated tessellated patterns and colours. Exterior tiles can be used for driveways and paths, in courtyards, on patios, terraces and verandahs, and around swimming pools. Made from concrete or clay, they come in a variety of colours, sizes and finishes.

• Concrete tiles, made from finely crushed aggregate, are fired at extremely high temperatures and are usually quite thick (approximately 15–20 mm), with a variety of texture finishes to replicate natural products. They have low porosity and high impact-resistance, and offer a range of tessellating options when laid. Colours usually vary between batches, so when purchasing try to ensure your order is filled from a single source.

• Clay (or ceramic) tiles have been popular for years in many situations, both inside and out. Those suited to exterior use include terracotta and quarry tiles.

Quarry tiles have a rough surface, making them non-slip in exposed weather situations. Tiles made from terracotta (which is Italian for 'baked earth') have a porosity higher than that of concrete tiles, meaning they are more absorbent, a problem particularly around barbecues. Generally, their rough surface and fade-resistant, rich, earthy colours make them a popular choice for exterior use.

The usual thickness of quarry tiles is 15 mm, but irregularities can sometimes occur. To maintain the non-slip quality and avoid trapping discolouration, leave terracotta tiles unsealed outdoors.

COMBINATIONS

Many paved areas in the garden may combine two or more of the previously mentioned materials. A combination such as limestone pavers with a terracotta header or stone with a brick border will create an unusual yet harmonious result in the garden.

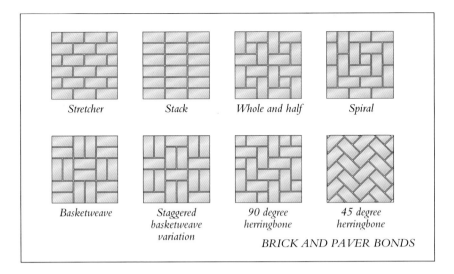

Stretcher Stack Whole and half Spiral

Basketweave Staggered basketweave variation 90 degree herringbone 45 degree herringbone

BRICK AND PAVER BONDS

BONDS

STACK
Stack is an easy bond to lay, but take care to maintain straight lines in both directions. This does not provide a strong bond and is unsuitable for driveways.

STRETCHER
Stretcher creates a strong bond which looks best as a meandering path between two header courses. It is also useful on large straight areas and curves, and in unusual layouts.

HERRINGBONE
Herringbone is a strong, interlocking style that is particularly good for driveways and other high-use areas. The pattern fits easily into irregular shapes and tends to make paved areas look longer. If herringbone bond is laid at 45 degrees, you will need to cut a lot of bricks. Plan the layout carefully to ensure this time-consuming process is minimised.

BASKETWEAVE
Visually, this repeating pattern tends to 'close in' and reduce the apparent size of paved areas. It is most appropriate in square or rectangular situations, as difficult cutting is required when adapting basketweave to curved edges.

SPIRAL
Spiral is an active pattern, creating movement from the centre.

PROVIDING AN EDGE
Any paved area requires an edge. Whether to lay this edge first or last is a personal decision often regulated by the material and pattern selected. The edge provides a perimeter to contain the paving, retain bedding sands and loose material, delineate other areas

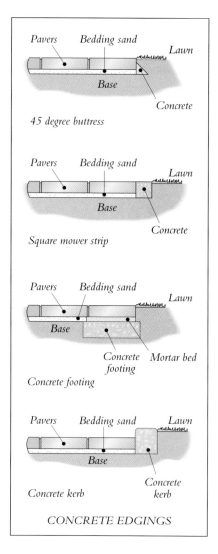

45 degree buttress

Square mower strip

Concrete footing   Concrete   Mortar bed
                    footing

Concrete kerb   Concrete
                 kerb

CONCRETE EDGINGS

sides, is called the 'header course'. A header course, constructed with whole bricks which fully contain any smaller cut sections, strengthens the edge of the paving and adds a decorative finish when laid in a contrasting colour.

A square header course is laid at right angles to the paving; a longitudinal header course or 'soldier course' is laid parallel.

Raised brick edging acts as a kerb to retain garden beds or direct the flow of water.

CONCRETE EDGING
Driveway, path and courtyard surfaces often meet gardens or lawns and need strong edges to prevent movement, as any loss of soil from beneath the base eventually causes paving to sink.

• Create a buttress of 45 degrees. After laying your paving with brick or stone, cut away and remove any loose material down to the firm base. Place concrete against the edge bricks and, using a metal or wooden float, batter it at an angle of 45 degrees to form a buttress. The concrete should cover at least half the depth of the bricks. Once the light covering of topsoil is returned, surrounding plants or lawn can grow up to the edge of the paving.

• Install a square mower strip, formed in a similar way to a buttress.

• Include a concrete footing, enabling the concrete to be hidden from view while still acting as a retainer.

(such as garden beds) and even double as a mowing strip at the side of a lawn.

BRICK EDGING
The edge on brick paving, placed either square or lengthwise down the

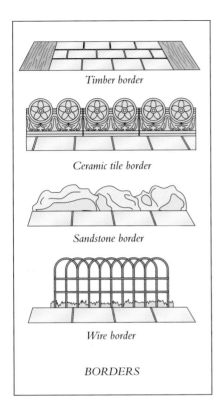

Timber border

Ceramic tile border

Sandstone border

Wire border

BORDERS

• Construct a concrete kerb to redirect water flow and/or retain an area higher than the paving.

TIMBER EDGING

Timber edging is useful for retaining loose paving materials such as bark and pebbles. Lay durable hardwood or preservative-treated pine with a C24 rating lengthwise along the path and fix it into position with wooden pegs and galvanised nails. Old railway sleepers can be laid to form retaining walls or seating. Drive the pointed ends of treated pine logs into the ground to form a vertical barrier.

TERRACOTTA TILE EDGING

Decorative terracotta edging tiles, which stand vertically and form interesting patterned edges, are enjoying a resurgence.

Rectangular border tiles are often used like a header course. A border of a different colour or with an inlaid frieze provides visual impact when used in moderation.

STONE AND ROCK EDGING

Rock and stone are excellent as hard edging and work equally well with paths of loose material, stepping stones and bricks. Stone or rock is effective along free-flowing and curved paths.

ALTERNATIVE EDGINGS

Historical influence or the unavailability of traditional materials in some areas prompts innovative approaches to edging. Glass, in the form of bottles (particularly large dark-coloured beer or wine bottles), is sometimes used as edging and in retaining walls. To construct a glass edge, stand the bottles vertically upside down and push them firmly into the soil, supported by a 45 degree concrete buttress. Be wary of using glass in areas accessible to children or where the bottles may be broken accidentally.

Victorian and Edwardian garden beds were edged with loops of wire. Today, these looped and woven wire borders are available in rolls of galvanised or PVC- or powder-coated wire in a range of colours.

Slabs of slate laid randomly in the popular 'crazy paving' style coordinate beautifully with traditional clay pavers around this freeform swimming pool. Thorough preparation is vital when attempting an advanced design.

Paving techniques

Whatever you decide to pave, the basic steps remain the same. In any project, the keys to success are careful planning and solid preparation of the site; paving is only ever as solid as its base.

CALCULATING AREA

Most paving materials are sold by the square metre (m^2).

SQUARE OR RECTANGULAR AREAS

Multiply the length by the width. For example, the surface area of a courtyard that measures 12 m long by 5 m wide equals:

$12 \times 5 = 60 \ m^2$

To determine the number of bricks required, multiply the surface area (m^2) by forty (forty being the number of standard bricks to the square metre), thus:

$60 \times 40 = 2400$ bricks

CIRCULAR AREAS

Use the formula πr^2, where π equals 3.14 and r is the radius. For example, calculate the surface area of a paved circular feature with a radius of 4 m as follows:

$\pi \times r^2 = 3.14 \times 4^2 = 3.14 \times 16 = 50.24 \ m^2$

TRIANGULAR AREAS

When working with a triangle, multiply half the base length by the height. For a triangular area 4 m wide at the base and 6 m high, the calculation is:

$(\frac{1}{2} \times 4) \times 6 = 2 \times 6 = 12 \ m^2$

BASIC TOOLS

- String line
- Measuring tape
- Spirit level
- Straight-edge
- Shovel
- Spade
- Rake
- Hammer
- Rubber mallet
- Hand saw
- Screed rails and board
- Steel float
- Permanent black marking pen
- Club hammer
- Bolster chisel
- Wheelbarrow
- Broom
- Hose and nozzle

COMBINATION AREAS

For areas involving a combination of shapes, calculate each component individually, then simply add the totals together. For example, if the area of a terrace comprises a square and a triangle, sketch the area and divide it with a dotted line (see Combination areas, page 76).

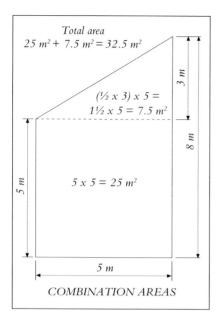

Total area
$25\ m^2 + 7.5\ m^2 = 32.5\ m^2$

$3\ m$

$(\frac{1}{2} \times 3) \times 5 =$
$1\frac{1}{2} \times 5 = 7.5\ m^2$

$8\ m$

$5\ m$

$5 \times 5 = 25\ m^2$

$5\ m$

COMBINATION AREAS

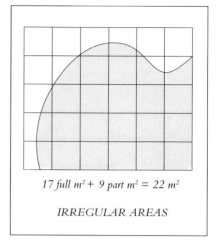

$17\ full\ m^2 + 9\ part\ m^2 = 22\ m^2$

IRREGULAR AREAS

Calculate the square area:
length x width = $5 \times 5 = 25\ m^2$
then calculate the triangular area:
$\frac{1}{2}$ base x height = ($\frac{1}{2} \times 3) \times 5 = 1.5 \times 5 = 7.5\ m^2$
As the final step, add the two area subtotals together:
$25\ m^2 + 7.5\ m^2 = 32.5\ m^2$

IRREGULAR AREAS
Estimate irregularly sized areas by sketching the outline of your proposed paving carefully on to squared paper, with each square representing 1 m^2, as shown in the diagram above right.
Add up the whole square metres:
$m^2 = 17$
Even-out the part-square metres by combining them:
$m^2 = 5$

Always round partial metres up to a full metre to allow for wastage from cut or broken pavers. Thus:
$17 + 5 = 22\ m^2$

ORDERING MATERIALS
Shop around for the best value on price or look for discounted products.
• Builders merchants sell house bricks and clay and concrete pavers. Original sandstocks and footpath paving bricks are sometimes available second-hand from demolition yards. These are sold by the square metre or by the thousand. When converting from one to the other, remember that there are 40 standard house bricks per square metre. Thus: 1000 bricks/40 = $25\ m^2$
• Tiles and slate are sold by the square metre. Select only tiles suitable for exterior use if your paving will be exposed to the weather.
• Sandstone can be purchased new, secondhand or in an artificial form.

Ensure the stone chosen for your project is at least 50 mm thick.

• Various other materials (such as limestone pavers) are available from landscape and paving supply centres.

• Bedding material, usually in the form of sand, can be ordered by the tonne or by the cubic metre. A rule-of-thumb correlation is 1.5 tonnes to 1 m^3 of bedding sand. The material should be either coarse and natural (such as washed river sand) or a manufactured by-product of quarry crushing processes (packing sand).

To calculate your order, multiply the square metre surface area by the depth of the bedding. For example, when laying a 25 mm bed over an area of 20 m^2, calculate:

20 m^2 x a depth of 0.025 m = 0.5 m^3 then apply the rule-of-thumb correlation:

0.5 m^3 x 1.5 = 0.75 tonnes Double-check your calculations, then order a little extra to allow for slight variations in the depth of your bed.

• The ultimate base material for paving is concrete. Ready-mixed concrete is sold by the cubic metre (m^3). To calculate your needs, multiply the surface area by the depth proposed (usually 100 mm). For example, a rectangular area 12 x 5 m requires:

12 x 5 x 0.1 = 6 m^3 An alternative to concrete is a base of crushed rock, sold by the tonne through landscape supply centres or directly from quarries. To order, calculate the cubic metres required

(as for concrete), then multiply this by 1.5 to give an approximate tonnage (as for bedding sand). Thus:

12 m x 5 m x 0.1 m = 6 m^3, and 6 m^3 x 1.5 = 9 tonnes This type of base is considerably cheaper than concrete (about 20 per cent of the cost), but it does have to be compacted thoroughly to reduce the risk of future sinkage.

• You may need small amounts of other materials, including washed beach sand and cement, for grouting, and concrete for edging.

MIXING CONCRETE

Order concrete ready-mixed or mix it on site by hand. The most common blend comprises four parts coarse aggregate (gravel), two parts fine aggregate (preferably river sand), one part cement, and sufficient water to produce a workable consistency.

Coarse aggregate (in sizes of up to 20 mm) gives concrete its strength but for convenience use the 10 mm size, as this is easier to work.

If you require a large volume or do not want to mix your own, contact a local supplier ahead of time. Ready-mixed concrete is delivered in increments of 0.2 m^3. For example, standard quantities include 1.2 m^3, then 1.4 m^3, 1.6 m^3 and so on.

There are various standards that control the composition of ready-mixed concrete. For exposed paths, driveways and slabs not supporting structures, a strength of 15–20 newtons is required. To order concrete for this kind of paving base,

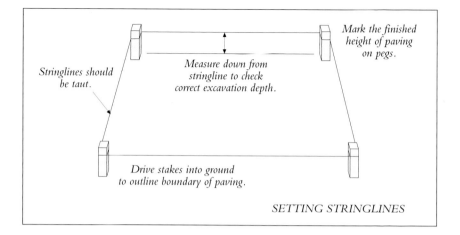

Stringlines should be taut.

Measure down from stringline to check correct excavation depth.

Mark the finished height of paving on pegs.

Drive stakes into ground to outline boundary of paving.

SETTING STRINGLINES

request a mix that conforms to either Gen 3 or ST4 (both of which have a minimum amount of 20 kg cement per cubic metre).

CALCULATING QUANTITY

Concrete quantities are calculated by the cubic metre (m^3).

Usually, 1 m^3 quantity of concrete comprises 1 m^3 of coarse aggregate, 0.5 m^3 of fine aggregate, eight bags of cement and water as required.

The area covered is determined by the thickness of the slab. For example, when laid to a depth of 100 mm, 1 m^3 covers 10 m^2.

To calculate concrete by volume, multiply the length by the width by the depth of the given area. For a 10 x 1.5 m slab 0.1 m deep, you require 1.5 m^3.

Typically, this quantity is made up of:
- 1.5 m^3 of coarse aggregate
- 0.75 m^3 of fine aggregate
- twelve bags of cement
- water as required

MARKING OUT

Mark out the area, placing a peg in each corner or at each change of angle. On the pegs, indicate the desired finished height of the paving material.

Consider the slope of the land to ensure the finished paving drains adequately in the desired direction. Sloping or ramped sites pose few problems (ramped areas having natural run-off) but if your site is level you must create crossfall on the area to displace water quickly while controlling its flow. Usually a fall of 20 mm per metre is sufficient.

COPING WITH A SLOPE

If your site is not level and is too steep for ramping, introduce steps.

When deciding whether a ramp or series of steps is needed, calculate the rate of incline. Measure the length of the area, then run a stringline from one end to the other, fixing it at ground level at the high point.

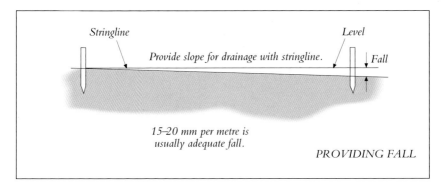

Stringline

Level

Provide slope for drainage with stringline.

Fall

15–20 mm per metre is usually adequate fall.

PROVIDING FALL

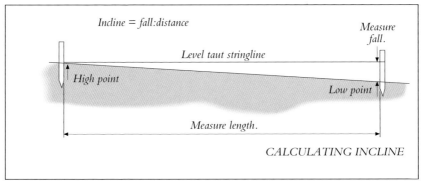

Incline = fall:distance

Measure fall.

Level taut stringline

High point

Low point

Measure length.

CALCULATING INCLINE

Stretch the stringline taut and horizontal. At the low point, measure the distance from the stringline to the ground to determine the amount of fall. Compare that to the distance, to obtain the rate of incline. As a guide, ramps may be used when the rate does not exceed 1:10 (that is, a 1 m fall over a 10 m length of path). If the slope is greater than 1:10, it is usually more appropriate to build steps.

EXCAVATION AND BASE PREPARATION

Having set the finished-height stringlines, excavate the area to the appropriate depth. Stretch a taut stringline from one side to the other at the desired paving edge height. Measure from the stringline to the surface, adjusting the soil as required.

Once the excavation is complete, check that the base is solid. If you locate soft spots, particularly in clay-based soils (due to poor drainage or broken pipes), dig them out. Redirect drainage or repair broken pipes before paving begins. Alternatively, rake cement through the existing base material, compact it firmly, hose the surface lightly and allow it to set.

Always work on a solid base to reduce the threat of future sinkage. Paving that carries only pedestrian traffic rarely requires a concrete or compacted base; unless the soil is clay-based and has drainage problems, simply lay the paving material straight on to a 25–50 mm depth of screeded bedding sand.

SCREEDING

Screeding is the technique of levelling bedding sand to remove the dips and bumps that would otherwise give the paving an uneven surface.

RAISED RAIL METHOD

Place timber edges or rails at the finished stringline height and peg or nail them into position. Select a straight piece of timber (usually 100 x 50 mm in dimension) long enough to cover the width of the area to be screeded. Cut a notch from each end, 8–10 mm shallower than your chosen paver. (This allows for compaction once the paving is in use.) Draw the screed board along the rails. Ensure the bedding is packed firmly. Use a metal float to push back or remove the build up of sand that occurs behind the board.

BEDDED RAIL METHOD

This is probably the easier method, as less preparation and fewer materials are required.

Use screed rails made from aluminium or PVC conduit, water pipe, or timber, bedded into the sand. (For narrow areas, only one rail is necessary.) Ensure the rails are below the finished string height by the same thickness as that of your bricks, less 8–10 mm. (Check this by placing one of your selected bricks on a screed rail and measuring its height against the stringline. The top should protrude 8–10 mm.) Drag a straight piece of timber or large spirit level steadily along the rails, screeding off and packing the sand to create a firm, level laying surface. Finally, remove the rails and use a float to fill the grooves with sand.

CURVED PAVING

Curves soften the landscape, invite leisurely, relaxed movement and make areas appear longer, particularly when you walk or glance down a meandering path, around a swimming pool or along a driveway.

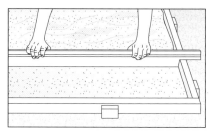

Draw a notched screed board along two raised rails. Ensure the bedding sand is packed firmly.

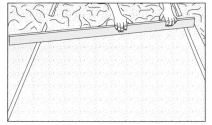

Bed the screed rails into the sand. Draw a straight-edge or spirit level along the rails, levelling the surface.

Curves are also useful for their capacity to work within an established garden landscape, accommodating obstacles such as rocky outcrops and large trees or shrubs you don't want to move.

If you choose to create a curved driveway, allow space for drivers to manoeuvre vehicles. Sharp curves are not compatible with areas demanding sweeping movement and parking or reversing bays.

Form rectangular or square pavers into a natural, free-flowing shape by including a header course – a border separate to the paving and laid, therefore, at any angle. If you want your paving to reflect a curve, choose stretcher bond as your pattern. This eliminates cutting as the pattern bends to follow the paving line. In other common patterns, the bulk of the paving is laid independently of the header, which follows a scribed curve.

FOLLOWING A CURVE

Position a length of hose or rope as a guide. Look at the curve from all angles, adjusting it until you are satisfied that any straight spots have been removed.

Lay the header bricks on one side, following the curve created by your line. Use this as a laying guide for the remainder of your paving, following the curved header with stretcher bond.

Lay the stretcher courses evenly, checking the lines and adjusting the joints to keep the curve smooth.

PAVING TO A CURVE

This method involves considerable cutting but allows you to choose from a wide variety of patterns and is suitable for areas of any size. With the exception of swimming pools, for which the header is laid first, large areas of paving are completed before the curved header is put into place.

Lay the paving to just past the boundary of your intended edging. Use a hose or length of rope to create a free-flowing curve across the surface. With a permanent marking pen, scribe this line on to the pavers.

Remove any surplus paving from outside the curve, then lift the marked pavers, numbering each paver to simplify the replacement process. Cut the pavers neatly where marked and reposition them in sequence, using the numbers as a guide.

Place your chosen header pavers around the curve, ensuring the back edge of each is aligned with the cut edge.

CIRCULAR PAVING

Paving circular areas can be more difficult and is usually more time-consuming than working with standard rectangular shapes.

Setting up requires careful planning, patterning is more complicated, and the need for careful brick-cutting is increased. Perseverence is rewarded, as circular paving looks fabulous when completed, but before attempting a circular design, make sure you obtain

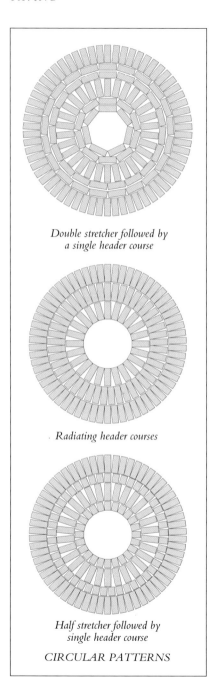

*Double stretcher followed by
a single header course*

Radiating header courses

*Half stretcher followed by
single header course*

CIRCULAR PATTERNS

some practical experience with basic paving techniques.

Circular courtyards or features between two or more radiating paths form focal points in the landscape. Sketch ideas on to paper and construct a sample to make sure your plan is feasible. Patterns that work effectively in circular areas include radiating headers, a single header plus a double stretcher, and crazy paving in stone.

LAYING THE PATTERN
The two basic methods for laying circular paving are outside-in and inside-out.

• To pave outside-in, place a peg at the centre of the site and attach a stringline to a nail at the top. With the string held taut, use a stick tied to the end to scribe a circle on the base. Beginning at the scribed line, work inwards. As the design tightens towards the centre, cut your bricks or pavers, if desired, or leave the area unpaved (and, perhaps, filled with plants) as a centrepiece.

• Inside-out paving is the more difficult method as it involves working in the confined space of the centre with your supply of materials outside the circle. Screed the area, then lay a plank across the sand as a makeshift walkway to provide access to your materials. Alternatively, you can avoid disturbing a screeded area by completing one full half of the circle before starting on the other section. Make sure that the halves match up exactly.

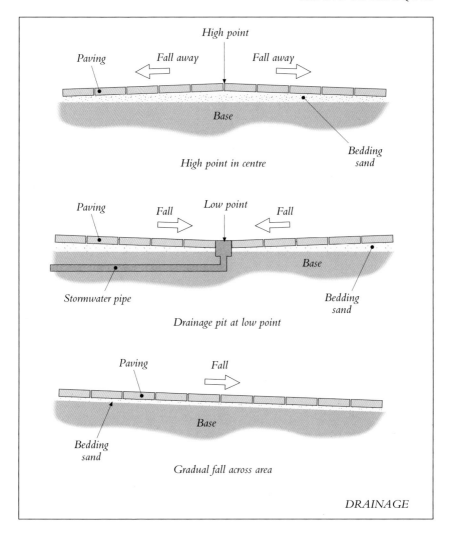

High point

Paving   Fall away   Fall away

Base

High point in centre

Bedding
sand

Paving   Fall   Low point   Fall

Base

Stormwater pipe

Bedding
sand

Drainage pit at low point

Paving   Fall

Base

Bedding
sand

Gradual fall across area

DRAINAGE

DRAINAGE FOR CIRCLES

Without correct fall, surface water will pool in the centre of your paving, making the area impractical for users and encouraging sinkage.

• On a level site, make the centre of the circle the high point, providing an even degree of fall away in all directions. Manipulate the fall by adding extra bedding material where required to create a gentle slope.

• On a sloping site, create a gradual fall across the width of the area.

• As an alternative on sloping ground, make the centre of the circle the low point and install a drain and subterranean pipework to remove excess water.

Pavers in light-traffic areas such as patios can be laid on a relatively inexpensive base of sand. Occasional sweeping with a stiff-bristled brush or broom is usually all that's required by way of maintenance.

Clay paving on sand

Laying pavers on a simple bed of sand is appropriate in areas that carry pedestrian traffic (such as paths, courtyards, barbecue areas, shady spots, patios and terraces).

PREPARATION

It is not necessary to place a base material beneath bedding sand provided the area drains freely and does not contain reactive, clay-based soil. A 45 degree buttress of concrete, suitable for most paving jobs, is one of the simplest edges to install.

1 Mark out the area, allowing for sufficient fall (preferably away from the house and towards grass, gardens, kerbs or drainage systems).

2 Set stringlines to the finished height (see page 78).

3 Excavate below the stringlines to at least 75 mm for clay pavers or 100 mm for house bricks.

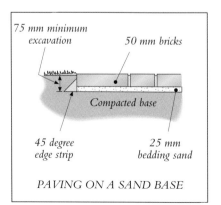

75 mm minimum excavation

50 mm bricks

Compacted base

45 degree edge strip

25 mm bedding sand

PAVING ON A SAND BASE

MATERIALS

- Clay pavers (or house bricks)
- Coarse-grained bedding sand
- Concrete mix for edging
- Fine-grained sand and/or soil for grout
- Cement

TOOLS

- Basic tool kit (see page 75)
- Brick saw or angle grinder for cutting bricks (optional)

4 Spread a 25 mm depth of bedding sand and rake it until it is roughly level. Screed using the method most suited to your work site (see Screeding, page 80).

LAYING

5 Laying pavers from an appropriate point saves a lot of cutting later. For example, if the proposed paving travels along two walls of your home and around a square corner, work outwards in both directions from the corner to avoid the cutting nightmare created by having a pattern meet there. Lay pavers against solid structures first, then proceed out

into an open space, again to prevent having to cut the final row.

6 Set up taut stringlines to guide your paving. Measure a small, loosely laid sample area to determine an accurate spacing.

7 If practical, lay a header course to provide a starting point (see Providing an edge, pages 71–3.)

8 Always lay pavers to set stringlines – do not simply butt them up to one another. Leave a small gap to accommodate variations in paver dimensions and keep the lines straight. Pavers need room for expansion and movement, so create a joint of 1–2 mm. Fit the pavers loosely to allow for minor adjustments and grouting.

CUTTING

9 Once all the pavers are in place, you may be left with space to be filled to complete the pattern. Before cutting a paver, mark it clearly. Place the paver across the space so that it sits on the surrounding surface.

Scribe a line at the correct angle, approximately 5 mm in from what you consider to be a tight fit.

10 Cut the paver using a bolster and club hammer, a block splitter, an angle grinder with a masonry blade or a brick saw.

• If using a bolster chisel and club hammer, place the paver on a firm bed of sand and tap around the four sides until it cracks.

• Block splitters or guillotines work best with cobblestones or house bricks, the compression action of the splitter tending to shatter pavers of baked clay.

• It is difficult to keep angle grinder cuts straight. To solve the problem, support each paver within a framework. Cut part-way through the paver, place a bolster in the cut and tap sharply with a lump hammer to create a clean break.

• Brick saws with diamond-tipped blades are ideal for cutting large numbers of pavers quickly and neatly. Hire a saw on a four-hourly or daily basis. To avoid excessive charges, have your material marked

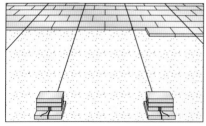

8 Always lay pavers carefully to set stringlines – do not simply butt them up to one another.

11 Insert each part-paver into the appropriate space, with the cut edge facing the header course.

ready for cutting before collecting the machine.

• Use a scutch hammer to trim the cut surfaces of soft house bricks.

11 Insert each part-paver into its space with the cut edge facing the header course.

COMPACTING

12 Check that the line of pavers is straight and make your final adjustments. Compact the paving by hand or machine. Use a piece of timber or other straight-edge as an anchor to hold the edge pavers in place, to prevent them moving.

EDGING

13 With a spade or float, cut the bedding sand away from the edge pavers, exposing the solid base.

14 Mix up a quantity of concrete.

15 Shovel concrete along the exposed paver edge.

16 Use a float to batter the mixture to a 45 degree angle, ensuring it

---

covers at least half the thickness of each paver. Allow the concrete to set completely.

GROUTING

17 Use a fine-grained washed beach sand, sifted soil or a combination of six parts sharp sand to one part dry cement between the pavers. Ensure the paving is dry, then throw the grout mix over the surface.

18 Use a firm-bristled broom to push the grout into the joints. Sweep away the excess, reserving it for topping up the joints as required at a future date. (When cement powder is included, finish the process by hosing the surface with a very fine spray of water.)

12 Check that the line of pavers is straight and make your final adjustments. Compact the paving.

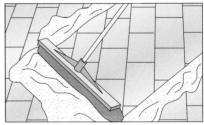

18 Use a broom to push the grout into the joints. Reserve the excess for topping up at a future date.

Clay paving on crushed rock

Heavy traffic areas such as driveways require the stability provided by a crushed rock base. This method is also suitable for land with drainage problems or reactive clay-based soils.

PREPARATION

In areas such as driveways, carports, swimming pools and moisture-laden spots with poor drainage, lay a solid base material beneath bedding sand. Crushed rock (known as hardcore) is about one-fifth the cost of concrete.

1 Mark out the area, allowing for sufficient fall (see pages 78–9).

2 Set stringlines and excavate.

3 Spread hardcore to a depth of approximately 100 mm. Rake or screed the surface. Measure the base height against the stringline and adjust the level of filling if necessary.

4 Hose the area lightly to moisten the surface and minimize dust.

TOOLS

- Basic tool kit (see page 75)
- Brick saw or angle grinder for cutting bricks (optional)

MATERIALS

- Clay pavers or house bricks
- Bedding sand
- Hardcore
- Concrete mix for edging
- Fine-grained sand for grout
- Cement

5 Compact the hardcore by machine.

6 Hose the area thoroughly and allow it to dry. When dry, the base should be almost rock hard.

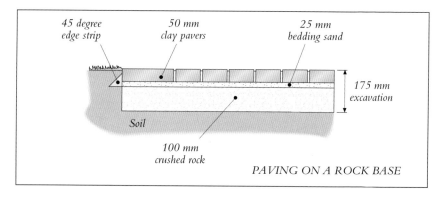

45 degree edge strip

50 mm clay pavers

25 mm bedding sand

175 mm excavation

Soil

100 mm crushed rock

PAVING ON A ROCK BASE

Laying clay pavers or bricks on a base of crushed rock eliminates the threat of contact with reactive clay-based soils, and minimizes the possibility of sinkage on poorly drained land.

7 Spread bedding sand over the base to a depth of approximately 25 mm. Rake until roughly level, then screed using your preferred method.

PAVING
8 Follow standard procedures for laying, cutting, compacting, edging and grouting (see Clay paving on sand, pages 85–7).

HINT

Crushed rock is both dense and heavy, which makes it difficult to shovel and barrow into position.
 If your area is large, follow the lead of the professionals and hire a bobcat digger to move and spread your base.

A solid concrete slab provides the ultimate base for clay paving. Not only does concrete insulate pavers against the soil, it helps prevent upheaval by tree roots and sinkage due to waterlogging should a nearby drainage pipe begin to leak.

Clay paving on concrete

Pave on a base of concrete for extra stability around swimming pools, along driveways and in parking bays and problem drainage areas. Plan to allow adequate curing time for the slab.

TOOLS

- Basic tool kit (see page 75)
- Jointing tool
- Pliers
- Cement mixer (if mixing your own)
- Square-nosed shovel
- Gumboots
- Edger
- Wooden float

MATERIALS

- Clay pavers or house bricks
- Timber formwork
- Timber pegs
- Nails
- 75 mm expansion material (such as Brickfill)
- A142M reinforced mesh, plus mesh men
- Tie wire
- Concrete
- Fine-grained sand or grout

HINT

When ordering ready-mixed concrete, ensure adequate access is available for its delivery and that a clear wheelbarrow track is available from the driveway to the intended work site. Remove any obstacles which might hinder easy transportation of the load.

PREPARATION

1 Mark out the area, allowing for sufficient fall in the desired direction (preferably away from buildings).

2 Set stringlines at the desired finished height. Excavate the area to a minimum depth of 175 mm when laying conventional clay pavers or 200 mm if you elect to work with standard house bricks.

3 Build the formwork (see Erecting formwork, page 92). For straight edges, use 100 x 50 mm or 75 x 50 mm timber. When following a curved design, use 100 x 10 mm pine offcuts which, although quite strong, are remarkably flexible.

4 If any part of the excavated area within the formwork is uneven and therefore requires filling, use clean sand screeded carefully to an appropriate level.

ERECTING FORMWORK

If your slab will rise above ground level, it will be necessary to construct formwork to contain the concrete. Formwork is a temporary structure, usually of timber or plywood, that holds wet concrete to the required shape until it has hardened.

Use long pieces of timber (such as oregon pine offcuts, which are flexible around curves), held in place with stakes on the outer sides. Use a spirit level to check that the formwork is level. Brace the formwork well to withstand the pressure of the heavy concrete.

5 If desired, place plastic sheeting into the excavation to prevent moisture rising through the concrete. This precaution is recommended for sheltered slabs, but is not necessary in exposed situations.

6 Place A142M reinforcing mesh into position inside the formwork.

Overlap the steel mesh by at least one-and-a-half to two squares and set it 50 mm in from the formwork edging. Join the mesh securely with tie wire, using a pair of pliers.

7 If laying a slab against brickwork or another solid structure, place an expansion material (such as Brickfill) against the wall at the finished concrete height. Fix this firmly in place by nailing through it and into a brick joint.

LAYING A SLAB

8 Move the concrete into position using a wheelbarrow. Once in place, spread and compact it using a square-nosed shovel.

9 Fill the excavation to the mid-way point. Lift the steel mesh to the surface of the still-wet slab and continue adding concrete until it reaches the desired level. As an alternative, support the steel mesh on reinforcement mesh men.

10 Using a shovel or sturdy bricklayers trowel, pack the wet

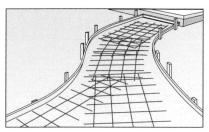

6 Place reinforcing mesh into position. Overlap the steel by at least one-and-a-half to two squares.

11 Move a straight-edge back and forth to level the concrete against the top of the formwork.

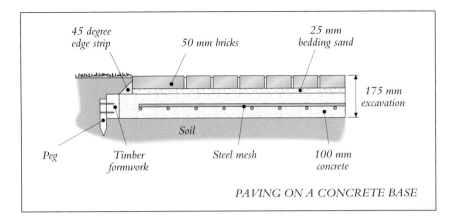

45 degree edge strip

50 mm bricks

25 mm bedding sand

175 mm excavation

Peg

Timber formwork

Soil

Steel mesh

100 mm concrete

PAVING ON A CONCRETE BASE

concrete tightly against the edges and into the corners of the formwork. Remove all air pockets.

11 Screed the concrete using a timber or aluminium straight-edge. Move the straight-edge slowly back and forth in a sawing motion to level the concrete against the top of the formwork, as though following the raised rail method (see Screeding, page 80). Do not edge the base slab.

12 Cut control joints to prevent uncontrolled cracking over time. Run grooves at regular intervals across the surface, using a straight-edge as a guide.

13 The surface of the concrete need not be particularly smooth. Finish the slab with a wooden float.

14 Allow the concrete to set and keep it wet for two or three days before removing the formwork.

PAVING

15 Lay clay pavers on to screeded bedding sand, or use flexible adhesive to attach them directly to the slab (see pages 190–5).

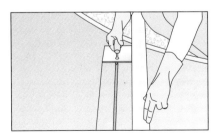

12 Cut control joints at regular intervals across the concrete surface, using a straight-edge as a guide.

13 The surface of the concrete need not be particularly smooth. Finish the slab with a wooden float.

Dry-bedding concrete pavers

Large pavers cover a surface area quickly and can be laid in a choice of ways. Pavers laid on a compacted base of crushed rock or concrete are easily bedded on coarse-grained sand.

MATERIALS	TOOLS
• 100 x 50 mm rails for formwork	• Basic tool kit (see page 75)
• A142M steel mesh and ties	• Bolt cutters or angle grinder
• Mesh men	• Brick saw
• Concrete	• Pliers
• Concrete pavers (400 x 400 x 40 mm)	• Buckets
	• Wooden float
	• Cement mixer
	• Squeegee
	• Rubber gloves

PREPARATION

1 Mark out and prepare the area (see Preparation, page 85).

2 The square format of large pavers limits possible patterns to stretcher or stack bond, with an optional inlay.

3 Set up stringlines and a grid to guide your paving, and establish a definite laying face (see Setting out, pages 193–4). When paving around a solid structure or square corner, always work outwards to avoid having to cut pavers to fill awkward spaces.

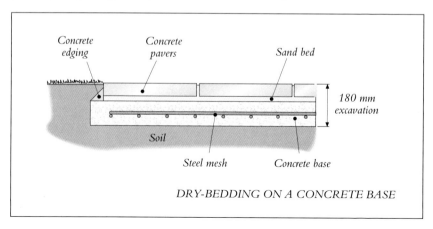

Concrete edging *Concrete pavers* *Sand bed*

180 mm excavation

Soil

Steel mesh *Concrete base*

DRY-BEDDING ON A CONCRETE BASE

Fine-grained sand is the only grout required in this waterside location, laid with imitation limestone pavers. The faux stone finish is just one of many developed by the manufacturers of modern concrete products.

4 Leave a 5–10 mm grouting joint. Use spacers cut from fibro cement or cardboard to keep the joints even.

5 Check the level, and tamp if needed.

LAYING THE PAVERS
6 Lay the full pavers first, then fill the remaining gaps with cut sections. For convenience, use a diamond-bladed brick saw when cutting heavy concrete pavers.

7 Grout with fine-grained, dry sand.

8 Compact with a plate vibrator, taking care not to damage the pavers.

9 Lay your choice of edging (see Providing an edge, pages 71–3).

Wet-bedding concrete pavers

Pavers laid on a solid concrete slab can be set on compacted sand or, preferably, wet-bedded for stability on to a base of freshly mixed mortar.

<table>
<tr><td>

MATERIALS

- 100 x 50 mm rails for formwork
- A142M steel mesh
- Ties and mesh men
- Concrete
- Sand and cement for mortar and slurry
- Concrete pavers (400 x 400 x 40 mm)
- Plasticizer

</td><td>

TOOLS

- Basic tool kit (see page 75)
- Bolt cutters or angle grinder
- Brick saw
- Pliers
- Buckets
- Wooden float
- Cement mixer (if mixing your own)
- Squeegee
- Rubber gloves

</td></tr>
</table>

PREPARATION
1 Mark out the area.

2 Excavate to a depth of 180 mm below the finished stringline height.

3 Set up formwork and pour the concrete. Allow the slab to dry.

4 Sweep the base and acid etch.

5 Set up stringlines and grids to control the laying sequence.

MIXING MORTAR
6 Mix a 3:1 mortar of three parts fine-grained washed sand to one part cement, with a plasticizer added.

7 Dampen the concrete and spread a slurry of six-parts cement to one-part sand, or sprinkle neat cement over the concrete and spray gently with water. Sweep the surface lightly.

8 Set up screed rails and level the wet mortar mix to a depth of 25–30 mm.

9 Sprinkle neat cement over the wet mortar, then moisten and trowel it.

LAYING THE PAVERS
10 Coat the back of each paver with slurry. Bed and tamp it into position to the finished stringline height.

11 Leave a 5–10 mm joint between the pavers for grouting.

12 Place a straight-edge over the surface to check for level.

Small concrete pavers set on a bed of wet mortar are easily manoeuvred into position to create several levels on sloping ground. In this courtyard, they provide a clean, dry surface in a naturally damp and shady spot.

13 Lay full pavers, then fill any remaining gaps with cut sections.

14 Allow the paving to dry for at least twelve hours, keeping it covered and moist to prevent cracking.

15 Prepare a grout mix, adding a colourant if desired, and mix it to a workable consistency.

16 Moisten the joints with a wet sponge and use a rubber squeegee to push the grout into place until it is flush with the tops of the pavers.

17 Remove excess grout and clean the pavers with a damp sponge.

18 Edge the paving with the method of your choice.

Concrete path

Concrete is a very adaptable construction material for paths as it can be formed into any shape desired. The wet concrete is held in place with formwork until it is dry. Once dry, concrete provides a solid walking surface that can be finished off in a variety of ways.

TOOLS

- Basic tool kit (see page 75)
- Pliers
- Concrete mixer (if mixing your own)
- Gumboots
- Skip float
- Edging tool
- Jointing tool (home-made)
- Wooden float

MATERIALS

- Concrete★
- Timber formwork (see step 5)
- Timber pegs
- Nails
- Reinforcing mesh (optional)
- Tie wire
- 75 mm expansion material

★ If mixing your own concrete, see steps 1–2; if ordering ready-mixed concrete, see box on page 100.

ORDERING CONCRETE

1 Concrete can be ordered ready mixed or be hand mixed on the job. If you want to mix the concrete yourself, be aware that there are different 'recipes' of concrete available for different jobs, whether for general purpose, foundations or paving. The recommended mix for paving consists of:

- 2½ parts coarse aggregate (gravel);
- 1½ parts fine aggregate (sand);
- 1 part cement;
- water to mix.

Rather than use separate sand and aggregate, you can buy 'combined aggregate', for which the mixture would be 1 part cement and 3½ parts 'combined aggregate'. You can also buy dry ready-mixed concrete (and mortar) to which you simply add water; this, however, is expensive for anything other than small jobs.

Small amounts of concrete can be mixed by hand on a large flat board. For quantities greater than 0.2 m³, you should consider hiring a concrete mixer, and for those greater than 0.5 m³ have concrete delivered ready mixed (see page 100).

Dry cement is usually purchased in 50 kg bags from builders' merchants or DIY outlets. Store the bags in a dry place off the ground, on pallets if possible, as the cement will harden if left on the ground or on concrete floors. It is best, however,

Concrete is a practical and economical pathway material, useful for lengthy paths. This concrete path has been jointed at regular intervals to prevent cracking and has been finished with a wooden float to give it a non-slip surface.

to buy only as much as you need, as cement can take in moisture from the air and can harden.

CALCULATING CONCRETE QUANTITIES

2 Concrete quantities are worked out by the cubic metre (m³). The area covered by a cubic metre is determined by the thickness of the slab. For example, if a slab is 100 mm thick, a cubic metre of concrete will cover 10 m². To calculate the amount of concrete you need, multiply length by width by depth. For example, a path that is 10 m long x 1 m wide x 100 mm deep would need 10 x 1 x 0.1 = 1 m³ of concrete.

ORDERING READY-MIXED CONCRETE

If your path requires a great deal of concrete (more than 0.5 m³) or if you do not want to mix your own, you can have it delivered by a lorry that is, in effect, a large concrete mixer on wheels.

When ordering ready-mixed concrete, check the minimum quantity the supplier will deliver (some have a minimum amount of 0.5 m³ or even 1 m³). Also make it clear what you want the concrete for, so that they can give you the correct mix.

The supplier will be able to tell you how long you have for barrowing the concrete from the lorry to the path (typically ½ hour per m³). You will certainly need to have everything ready, but check whether the supplier will provide his own wheelbarrows.

To order the materials required for a 1 m³ path (that is if you intend to hand mix your concrete), use the following quantities.

Concrete path (and all exposed paving)
- 8 bags cement
- 600 kg sand
- 1200 kg aggregate (or 1800 kg 'combined aggregate')

The corresponding figures (that is, per m³ of finished concrete) for the other two main types of concrete – general-purpose and foundation concrete – are as follows.

General purpose (most uses except foundations and exposed paving)
- 6½ bags cement
- 680 kg sand
- 1175 kg aggregate

Foundation concrete (foundations, footings, bases for pre-cast paving)
- 5½ bags cement
- 720 kg sand
- 1165 kg aggregate

PREPARATION

3 Make the initial preparations and lay out the path (see pages 75–81). This path is curved and 1.4 m wide.

4 Excavate and remove all vegetation to a depth of 100 mm below the finished height of the path.

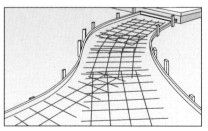

7 Place reinforcing mesh inside the formwork. Overlap the steel at least one and a half squares.

9 Spread out half the concrete; lift the steel mesh to the middle of the slab before adding the rest of the concrete.

5 Form up the timber edges to the predetermined levels. Give the path cross-fall to allow water to drain off. Peg and nail the formwork in position to create a strong edge, able to withstand the pressure of wet concrete. For straight edges, use either 100 x 50 mm or 75 x 50 mm timber. This curved path uses 100 x 10 mm timber offcuts, which are quite strong yet provide sufficient flexibility to shape the desired curve. The curves should be gradual, as tight curves are difficult to edge neatly.

6 If the area within the formwork needs filling, use sand which can be screeded off to the appropriate level (see Screeding, page 80). If preferred, place plastic sheeting under the concrete to prevent rising moisture, although this is not necessary under a path.

7 For added strength, place reinforcing mesh inside the formwork. (Concrete paths can be constructed without using steel mesh, but it will avoid the path cracking at a later date, particularly if the slab

10 Move the timber straight-edge back and forth in a sawing motion to level off the excess concrete.

thickness is only 75 mm.) Overlap the steel mesh at least one and a half squares and set it 50 mm in from the formwork edging. Tie the steel mesh together with tie wire, using pliers.

8 If the concrete is to be laid against brickwork or other solid structures, it is advisable to place an expansion material such as hardboard between the wall and the proposed area of concrete. To fix the expansion material firmly against the brickwork, nail through it and into a brick joint. Set the joint at the finished concrete height.

LAYING THE CONCRETE

9 If you have ordered ready-mixed concrete, ensure that a wheelbarrow track is available and clear of obstacles for ease of delivery. Barrow the mixed concrete into position, and then spread and compact it using a square-nosed shovel. Once half your required depth is reached, lift the steel mesh to the middle of the slab before adding more concrete to top up to the finished height. If required, add expansion joints on long paths (see page 102). Pack the concrete tightly into all edges and corners of the formwork.

10 Screed off the excess concrete using a timber or aluminium straight-edge. Move the screed board slowly back and forth in a sawing motion to level off the concrete with the top of the formwork.

EXPANSION JOINTS FOR LONG PATHS

Where a path is longer than 2 m, you will need an expansion joint to prevent the concrete cracking. Such a joint absorbs the movement of the material and should run at right angles to the path.

The simplest way of creating an expansion joint is to insert a strip of expansion material (hardboard), propping it vertically with mortar while you fill the area on either side with concrete. If reinforcing mesh is used you will only be able to use a half-thickness joint.

For very long paths, you should also add dummy joints between the main expansion joints. These will ensure that if the concrete does crack it will do so in a single place without ruining the appearance of the concrete.

To form a dummy joint, press a T-shaped metal section into the concrete, or make a special tool with a thin protruding blade, which you can draw along a timber straight-edge.

11 Move a skip float (or a long, narrow float) lightly over the area to push the aggregate down, and to smooth and 'cream up' the surface ready for trowelling. This technique brings the wet mix of sand and cement to the surface and pushes the aggregate deeper into the concrete.

12 Use a hammer or mallet and tap along the side edge of the formwork. This helps to settle the edge concrete and prevents honeycombing. It will also prevent the edge from dropping when the concrete is later edged.

13 Use a hand-held float to 'cream up' the edges and to pack them hard prior to edging.

14 Roughly edge the path with a 75 mm L-shaped edging tool to push the stones down. If this is not done before the concrete hardens, it will be difficult to achieve a neat edge.

ADDING DUMMY JOINTS
15 To make a dummy joint (see box on left), calculate the position of the joints and mark them on the

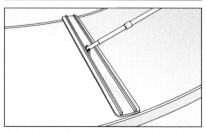

11 Move a large float over the surface to push the aggregate down and to smooth and 'cream up' the surface.

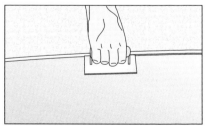

14 Roughly edge the finished path with a 75 mm edging tool to push the stones down.

formwork before pressing a T-shaped metal bar into the wet concrete. If using a jointing tool, place a straight-edge across the path on the marked position and hold the tool hard against the straight-edge.

FINISHING

16 Allow the concrete to dry to a point where only the surface is still workable. Generally this will take a few hours, depending on weather conditions. To finish the surface, use a wooden float and move it over the damp concrete in a circular motion to create a non-slip walking surface. (You can also use a broom, which will give you a grainier finish, or a steel float, for a smoother finish.)

17 Refinish the dummy joints and edging. The edging should be smooth with no breaks.

18 Allow the path to dry slowly. If concrete dries too quickly, cracks will appear in the surface. Keep the path moist for several days by covering it, or damping it with a hose to allow it to 'cure'.

Concrete can also be purchased ready made as square pavers, and laid in neat rows to make a wide path.

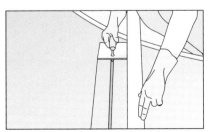

15 Hold a jointing tool hard against the straight-edge and cut a joint across the width of the path.

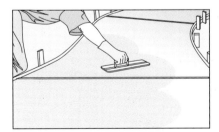

16 To create a non-slip surface, use a wooden float and move it over the damp concrete in a circular motion.

Stepping stone path

The use of stepping stones creates an informal and easy-to-construct path, which can be laid in straight or curved lines with equal ease. A stepping stone path is ideal for areas that are constantly moist or wet underfoot, or areas such as lawn that begin to show signs of wear from foot traffic.

METHOD

1 To lay timber rounds across a grassed area, step out the area where the path will be, marking each stride as the location for each round. Lay the rounds on the grass and walk across them to check the stride spacing. If necessary, adjust the distance between the rounds. Do not have them too far apart as this will make walking uncomfortable. If someone else is going to be using the path, it is a good idea to ask them to check the stride spacing for comfort also. As a general rule, the average adult stride is between 600 and 700 mm when measured from centre to centre.

2 With the timber rounds in place, examine the line taken by the path and adjust it until you are happy with the direction and shape.

3 Leave the rounds in place and cut around them with a spade or lawn edger. Remove each round and set it aside. Dig out sufficient soil to allow for the depth of the timber round,

1 Lay the timber rounds on the grass, and then check the stride spacing, adjusting the rounds if necessary.

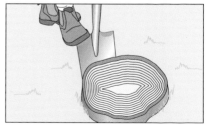

3 Leaving the timber rounds in place, use a spade or lawn edger to cut out the grass around them.

Stepping stones are suited for light traffic areas, such as a path leading to the clothes line or garden shed, and are less intrusive across a lawn than a path. The stones are set level with the ground to make lawn mowing easier.

plus approximately 50 mm of coarse-grained bedding sand.

4 Add the bedding sand and level the surface roughly with a float or trowel. Tamp the surface to ensure it is well compacted. Coarse-grained sand is a better bedding sand than some of the fine-grained sands, because it compacts to a firm base

4 Add 50 mm of coarse-grained sand and level the surface roughly with a float or trowel.

Concrete paving slabs are a good option for a stepping stone path. Here the thick plantings of grass give the path a less formal appearance, as the plants spill on to the pathway, softening the edges.

SELECTING STEPPING STONES

Stepping stones can be made from a variety of materials, all of which are laid on a sand bed.
- Precast concrete slabs are available in a variety of shapes and colours, and are well suited to a formal garden setting. Round, square, rectangular and kidney shapes are common and come in a range of sizes to suit the situation.
- Timber rounds look good in a natural setting. They are cut from a variety of hardwoods to a minimum thickness of about 50 mm. Softwood timber is not recommended, because direct ground contact will lead to rot, insect and fungal attack. To increase the life of the timber, coat the rounds with preservative

before laying them. Preservative-treated rounds can be purchased ready-cut. If you are able to obtain suitably-sized timber, cut your own stepping stones using a chain saw.
- A flagstone is any flat, irregularly shaped stone or rock. Although heavy and sometimes difficult to find, the natural colours and durability of this type of stone make it an excellent choice as a path material. When selecting stones, choose large pieces of similar thickness.
- For a more formal approach, create stepping stone pads from bricks laid at intervals. Usually two, three or four bricks are sufficient for each pad.

and, at the same time, provides good drainage qualities.

5 Place the round in position and tap the surface with a rubber mallet. Check the surface is level using a

spirit level. Continue in this manner until all the rounds are in position.

6 To complete the path, fill in around the edges of the rounds with clean soil plus grass seed.

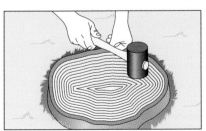

5 Place the timber round in position and tap the surface using a rubber mallet to settle it in place.

HINTS
- When laying in a lawn, make sure that the rounds or stones are settled at ground level for ease of mowing.
- If laying rounds or stones in a loose material path, raise them slightly so the gravel or bark does not scatter over them.

Sandstone paving

Sandstone can be laid on a variety of bases: a dry mix of six parts sand to one part cement; a 50 mm bed of dry, washed river sand; or a concrete slab, using wet mortar.

PREPARATION

1 Make initial preparations and lay out the area. In this example, a random pattern known as 'crazy paving' is used.

2 Excavate the site, remembering that extra depth may be required to allow for variations in the stone.

3 Compact the soil. If the ground is spongy or of highly reactive clay, excavate for a further 100 mm and lay a bed of crushed rock.

4 Spread and screed a 50 mm layer of coarse-grained bedding sand.

5 Set up stringlines (or use pieces of rope as a guide for a curve).

6 Group the sandstone into piles of varying thickness.

LAYING THE STONE

7 Lay a straight-edged section of sandstone against the guiding edge to neaten what is otherwise an informal jigsaw pattern. If possible, lay the outer edges first, positioning the largest stones around the sides to create maximum strength in the design. Smaller stones tend to move

TOOLS
● Basic tool kit (see page 75)
● Dust mask and goggles for dry cutting

MATERIALS
● Split sandstone
● Coarse-grained bedding sand
● Concrete mix for edging
● Cement for grout
● Fine-grained sand for grout
● Mortar

under pressure and are best laid towards the centre.

8 Use your sense of perspective to fit the puzzle together. Leave a gap of about 10–20 mm for grouting. Adjust

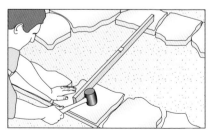

8 Tamp the pieces in place with a rubber mallet or softwood straight-edge and club hammer.

Sandstone is available in a choice of colours and patterns, ranging from subtle muted tones to this striking striated variation. It is most commonly laid in a random arrangement known as crazy paving, or as neatly sawn square blocks.

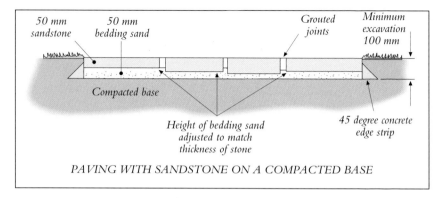

50 mm sandstone   *50 mm bedding sand*   *Grouted joints*   *Minimum excavation 100 mm*

Compacted base

Height of bedding sand adjusted to match thickness of stone

45 degree concrete edge strip

PAVING WITH SANDSTONE ON A COMPACTED BASE

the depth of the bedding to accommodate stones of various thicknesses. Tamp the pieces in place with a rubber mallet or softwood straight-edge and club hammer, taking care to avoid chipping. Mortar the pieces into position.

9 Fill any remaining gaps with smaller pieces of sandstone mortared into place. If trimming is required, use a hammer and bolster to maintain the split appearance; do not be tempted to cut the stone.

10 Check the finished level, then tamp the stone once more by hand.

11 Edge the area (see Providing an edge, pages 71–3).

12 Grout the freshly laid sandstone using one of two methods.
• Spread a dry mix of 6:1 fine-grained sand and cement and sweep it into the joints. Remove the excess and hose lightly with a fine spray.
• Mix a very stiff mortar and push it

neatly into the joints, using a trowel. Smooth with a small paintbrush moistened with fresh water. Clean the face of the sandstone with a large, lightly dampened sponge. Change the water regularly to prevent staining the stone.

HINT

Sandstone is heavy! For example, an 800 x 400 x 50 mm paving slab weighs approximately 38 kg. Sandstone is easiest to move and lay when two people work together, but remember to take care when handling the corners as they break off easily.

9 Fill any remaining gaps with smaller pieces of sandstone mortared into position.

SANDSTONE PAVING ON CONCRETE

No material surpasses solid concrete as a base for paving. Under sandstone pavers, the stability of a concrete slab prevents movement and cracking.

PREPARATION
1 Mark out the area, allowing for sufficient fall.

2 Set finished-height stringlines.

3 Excavate the site to a depth of approximately 180 mm.

4 Set up the formwork, place A142M steel mesh inside the area and pour the concrete.

5 Cut sandstone with a brick saw or hammer and bolster. If it is too thick to be split in the conventional manner, cut mid-way through each piece with a circular saw and masonry blade, then force the stone open with wedges or a bolster. As an alternative, lay the sandstone over a piece of metal angle-iron and tap the back until it splits.

Freshly sawn stone has sharp edges which must be rubbed with another piece of sandstone to prevent chipping.

MIXING MORTAR
6 Mix a mortar of 4:1 fine-grained sand and cement.

Add a plasticizer to make the mix light and workable.

7 Spread the mixture to form a 20–30 mm bed.

8 Dust the mortar with dry cement and wet the back of each sandstone piece with water or a bonding agent mixed with water.

LAYING THE STONE
9 Work outwards from a solid structure or corner, following perpendicular stringlines.

10 Align each stone carefully. Butt the pieces together, leaving a gap of 1–2 mm for expansion. Do not allow the edges or corners to touch as they chip easily. Lay the stones one row at a time. Move the stringlines regularly to check the alignment.

11 Adjust the stones by tamping with a softwood straight-edge and mallet to form an even surface. Check using a spirit level.

12 Edge the area with a material of your choice (see Providing an edge, pages 71–3).

13 Spread the area with fine-grained sand or a dry mix of 6:1 sand and cement, and sweep it into the joints.

Paving around pools

Bullnose coping pavers form a smooth, child-safe edging around swimming pools and formal ponds. Plan curved layouts carefully to ensure your chosen pattern fits neatly into the space provided.

CHOOSING MATERIALS

Square or rectangular pools have a formal appearance and look great set in cut stone, tiles, or clay or concrete pavers laid in regular geometric patterns. Free-flowing, natural-looking pools work well in a less formal setting of crazy paving, split stone, flagging or rumbled pavers.

Coping pavers are usually available in three basic shapes: half-bullnose, bullnose and coper.

POOL EDGES

The edging of a swimming pool can be either submerged or raised.

- Submerged edges lie below the waterline, creating a 'swim out' effect. As the selected paving material is constantly wet, special water-resistant adhesives are required. Consult your supplier for advice on fixing pavers under these conditions.
- Raised coping sits above the waterline in a step-like effect around the edge of the pool. Most pools are constructed in this way, with the paving fixed horizontally to a fibreglass or concrete surface. Choose an adhesive manufactured to withstand the constant lapping of water against the edge.

PREPARATION

1 Plan your paving to accentuate the pool's outline. Remember that achieving a neat finish is important. Pay particular attention to proposed cuts on corners and sharp curves.

2 Pre-cut your paving and lay out the coping. This is time-consuming, but potential problems can be corrected with relative ease at this early stage.

3 When laying raised coping over fibreglass, select an adhesive to suit both your paving material and the situation. These range from two-pack epoxy resins and solvent-based

Select a coping material and surround that blend harmoniously into the broader garden landscape. The warm-toned clay pavers in this setting complement the poolside collection of terracotta planters.

adhesives (such as Liquid Nails) for fibreglass to a 3:1 mix of sand and cement combined with a bonding agent for concrete. Consult your local supplier.

4 Improve keying by running a grinder lightly over the fibreglass to roughen the surface.

5 Identify a starting point. This can be anywhere around the side of an oval or round pool, but remember to manipulate the joint gaps in the last 2 m to eliminate unnecessary cutting. Rectangular or square pools are best worked from corner to corner. Pre-cut and lay the corners, then space the pavers evenly in between. Adjust the gaps to accommodate uncut, full pavers where possible. Treat irregularly shaped pools similarly, laying the corners first and modifying the joints to suit the pavers. If it is not possible to complete the design with full pavers alone, trim narrow widths from three or four pavers instead of removing a larger – and more noticeable – slice from just one.

LAYING

6 Mix the adhesive according to the manufacturer's instructions, and apply it to the top edge of the pool.

7 Press each paver into the adhesive, making sure the surface fall is away from the edging, to prevent loose debris entering the water. Allow the pavers to overlap the edge by

15–20 mm to minimize splash on to the surrounding surface.

8 From time to time, check the level.

9 Grout the joints either a section at a time or at the end.

10 Clean the surface of the pavers as you work, using a wet sponge and clean water. Remove all traces of adhesive and any mortar stains, and allow the paving to dry for twenty-four hours.

11 When you are sure the area is dry, paint the mortared joints with a bonding agent to seal them and prevent deterioration. Repeat this at regular intervals as part of your pool maintenance routine.

12 Once the coping is in place it provides an edge for the remainder of the pool surround. Prepare and pave this as you would any other open area, following the line of the coping with a suitable stretcher bond.

PAVING AROUND PONDS

The surround or edge of any pond can reflect either a formal or an informal design.

PREPARATION

Formal designs are built on regular geometric shapes, found in sandstone slabs, house bricks, clay pavers, slate pieces and tiles. Informal designs are accentuated by the rustic appearance of railway sleepers and the natural look of rock, cobbles and plants.

A pond used to attract wading birds or animal life requires a vastly different approach to that of one designed to withstand the pressure of humans walking or sitting on the edge.

In formal settings, the water level usually rests just below the edging. Ensure the capping material is parallel to the surface.

Use materials that blend with the landscape, or create contrast by choosing colours or textures that differ from those nearby.

It is difficult to mortar bricks, cut stone, tiles or slate directly to the plastic liners used in many ponds, so construct walls or footings of brick or concrete before laying the capping. Use a concrete footing which doubles as a floor to add stability beneath brick or concrete walls. Paint the inner surface with a waterproofing agent to seal the pond.

When mortaring a capping on to a pond wall, use a bonding agent in the mix to improve adhesion and waterproofing.

CHOOSING AN EDGING

As water often overlaps informal edges, the edging material is usually submerged. Use a plastic liner to create a natural-looking free-form pond. Position the perimeter of the liner above the anticipated water level before laying your chosen edging material around the side. Batter a buttress of concrete to hold it in place. Informal rock edges look natural as flowing curves. A partly submerged boulder adds interest at the water's edge.

Cut timber to any shape to create a useful edge where a pond surround is extended into a deck. Use timber vertically along the edges by setting treated logs on end in the ground.

Allow water to lap at natural-looking gravel or pebbles planted to harmonize with the landscape. Use rock or timber paving to strengthen soft edges to withstand foot traffic.

ADDING FEATURES

Install a small fountain, a statue, a running tap from a reticulating pump or a small bridge to give your project a professional finish.

A series of broad sandstone steps eases the transition from lawn to paved driveway on this sloping block. The uneven number and the depth of these steps make them both attractive and practical as a garden feature.

Paving steps

Whether designed to cope with a sloping site or to terrace a yard, steps or ramps add relief to the landscape. Choosing materials in keeping with the environment makes them less obtrusive.

TOOLS	MATERIALS
• Basic tool kit (see page 75)	• Clay pavers (or house bricks)
• Cement mixer (if mixing your own)	• Timber formwork
• Square-nosed shovel	• Timber pegs
• Wellington boots	• Nails
• Edger	• Concrete
• Wooden float	• Bonding agent

DESIGNING STEPS

When designing steps that will be functional and attractive, combine a 150 mm riser with a 350 mm tread. Provide a 5–10 mm fall to the front to prevent water pooling. (Modify these dimensions if desired.)

Gradual steps laid on gentle inclines can be fitted with treads deeper than the standard 350 mm, enabling walkers to step twice or more on each level. Steep steps are necessary on sharply inclining ground. Build these with one-step treads and install a handrail for safety.

Stepped ramps are appropriate on long, gentle inclines. Place risers vertically to break up the surface.

BUILDING A SINGLE STEP

1 Using 100 x 50 mm timber, form up the front and side edges of the step. Peg the timber formwork firmly into position.

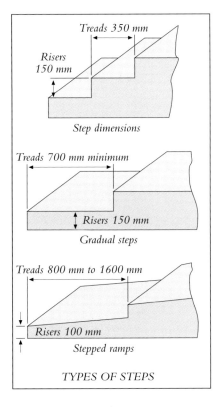

Step dimensions

Gradual steps

Stepped ramps

TYPES OF STEPS

2 Mix and pour the concrete to the top of the formwork. Level the surface with a wooden float, leaving a rough finish.

3 Allow the concrete to dry for two or three days, then remove the formwork boards.

4 To create a riser, butter the reverse face of a paver with mortar and tap it firmly into position against the vertical concrete face. Improve adhesion by painting the paver and concrete with a bonding agent and water mixed in equal parts.

5 Mortar the treads into position, creating a 5–10 mm fall to the front. Ensure the treads overhang their risers by 15–20 mm. Lay a second row of pavers, running in the opposite direction.

RAMPS

Ramps are an alternative to several steps when negotiating inclines or changes in level on sloping ground.

For the sake of safety and convenience, the length of a wheelchair ramp must vary depending on the rate of incline.

RATE OF INCLINE	RAMP LENGTH
1:33	25 m
1:20	14 m
1:14	9 m
1:8	1.25 m

The average ramp should be sloped at 1:14, to a length of 9 m. Refer to Building Controls guidelines for further information.

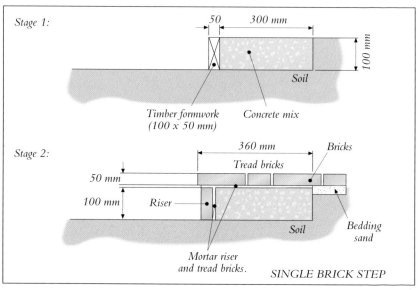

Stage 1:
50
300 mm
100 mm
Soil
Timber formwork (100 x 50 mm)
Concrete mix

Stage 2:
360 mm
Bricks
Tread bricks
50 mm
100 mm
Riser
Soil
Bedding sand
Mortar riser and tread bricks.

SINGLE BRICK STEP

WHEN TO USE A PROFESSIONAL

With enough time and motivation, it is possible to complete all the projects outlined in this book without needing to consult a professional. However, if you feel in doubt, do not hesitate to seek advice about some specific steps of your project. Here are some common problems and suggestions as to what you can do about them.

PREPARING THE SITE

Many projects don't even get started because the site seems unsuitable for the planned project. Sloping or uneven ground can be levelled for a paved area or path but, if preparation involves the removal or deposit of large amounts of soil, hire a machine, such as an excavator, to save time and energy. Check for drainage problems if the area often seems damp and, if necessary, consult a professional about installing drains and pipework.

LAYING CONCRETE

Concrete must be correctly mixed and then laid quickly before it sets. If you have a large area that you want to concrete, it is advisable to order the concrete ready-mixed from your local supplier. It is possible for you to hire tools for laying and finishing the concrete, but a professional will be much more familiar with their use, particularly when the concrete has to be laid over large areas.

CUTTING BRICKS AND PAVING TILES

Cutting the bricks and pavers to fill the final gaps can be a daunting task. If you don't feel confident enough to hire a brick saw and cut your own, take your carefully marked bricks to a brick or paver supply company. They will cut them for you (for a fee).

DIFFICULT PATTERNS

If you choose to lay a complicated tessellating pattern with tiles, you might need to consult a professional. This type of paving looks wonderful, but it does need a high degree of technical skill in order to produce a good result and to avoid both frustration and disappointment.

STEPS

Another area that may require professional assistance is the construction of formal steps from brick, tile or slate. This may depend on how many steps you want to build (more than three or four steps can be daunting), so weigh up your skills and the time that you have available before seeking help.

Loose materials

Paths can be constructed from a variety of loose materials, ranging from stone and gravel, to wood or bark chip, leaf mulch, or coarse and fine-grained sands. The materials are contained by lengths of treated softwood.

TOOLS

- Basic tool kit (see page 75)
- Spade

MATERIALS

- 75 x 50 mm preservative-treated softwood (rails)
- 75 x 50 mm preservative-treated softwood (pegs)
- 75 mm twisted, flat-head, galvanised nails
- Polythene sheeting (optional)
- Loose material

METHOD

1 Make the initial preparations and lay out the path (see pages 74–80 for details).

2 Set string lines at the finished height and spacing for the path. This path is 900 mm wide.

3 Remove all vegetation and excavate the proposed area to a depth of approximately 50 mm below the finished height of the path. Crown the base of the path, or provide cross-fall from one edging rail to the other to assist any water to drain away from the path.

4 Using a spade, dig a 20 mm deep trench along the string lines so that the pine edging will fit flush with the string line. Digging the edge rail into the base ensures that the loose material will not wash away from under the edge during heavy rain.

5 Form up edge rails to confine the path (see Cobbled path, page 128), using 75 x 50 mm timber, and fix with the pegs. Re-seal any cut surfaces to prevent the timber rotting when in contact with the ground). Alternative edges for confining loose materials include rock, sleepers, bricks, treated logs, stone or concrete kerbs.

6 Lay the polythene sheeting down between the timber edge rails to discourage weed growth.

7 Spread the loose material over the sheet, 50 mm deep, to bring it level with the top of the edging rails. Do not have too much depth as this will create more movement, making it difficult to walk along the path.

LAYING STEPPING STONES IN LOOSE MATERIAL

1 Excavate the entire path area and form up the edges with preservative-treated pine timber. Peg and fix in place.

2 Place the stepping stones of your choice in position, checking the stride spacing. If the stones seem at risk of movement, anchor them in place with a bed of mortar.

3 Fill around the stepping stones and up to the timber edging with a loose material of similar origin, such as timber rounds surrounded by bark chip, or concrete stepping stones surrounded by gravel. (An alternative is to set the stones close together and use any of the loose materials as infill for the small spaces that are left.)

This path uses a rough, stone-like, loose material. The raised edging prevents the stones from scattering over the lawn.

Stone and gravel path

This type of path is suited to both an informal and formal setting. The path is bordered on one side by split pieces of natural stone and is filled with coloured gravel.

METHOD
1 Make the initial preparations and lay out the path (see Path basics, pages 74–80).

2 Set your string lines, before excavating all vegetation to a depth of at least 100 mm below the finished string line height. If preferred, cover the path area with polythene sheet.

3 Cut the stone edging to a width of 200 mm, and to lengths of 500 mm and 250 mm (see box on Cutting stone, page 123).

4 Mix up enough mortar for bedding the border stones, using 3 parts sand to 1 part cement. Lay the sides of the path by bedding the stones firmly in mortar. Either leave a 20 mm gap between each piece of stone for mortar jointing (as for this path), or butt the stones together without a joint. Alternate the two sizes of stone along the path to add interest.

5 If you have left gaps, use a trowel to finish the joints with more of the same mortar mix. Use an old paint

4 Bed the stones along the sides of the path in mortar. Alternate the small and large pieces of stone.

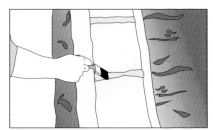

5 Fill gaps between the stones with mortar and smooth the surface with an old paint brush.

brush to smooth the surface of the mortar. Allow one or two days for it to dry.

6 Fill the area between the stone borders with gravel (approximately 50 mm deep), either matched to the colour of the stone or in contrasting, deeper shades. Rake the gravel in place and then tamp it until the surface is level and neat.

CUTTING STONE

If your stone is too thick to split with a hammer and bolster, cut halfway through from the stone's underside with either a brick saw, or angle grinder and masonry blade. Drive wedges or the bolster into the cut to force the stone to split in a rough manner.

Gravel is an inexpensive pathway material and is available in a variety of sizes and colours. This earth-coloured gravel teams beautifully with the cream-coloured stone running on one side and the brick wall on the other.

Brick and timber path

Wonderful paths can be created by combining a variety of materials. They can be a combination based on texture, colour or size. This rustic path is constructed using old house bricks and railway sleepers.

TOOLS

- Basic tool kit (see page 75)
- Circular saw
- Electric drill and bits

MATERIALS

- Old railway sleepers
- 75 mm (3 in) lost-head, galvanised nails
- Coarse-grained bedding sand
- Bricks
- Fine-grained sand
- Cement

LAYING THE SLEEPERS

1 Make the initial preparations and lay out the path (see the information on pages 74–80).

2 Set the string lines to the finished height and with an internal spacing between parallel sleepers of four brick lengths. To avoid cutting bricks, lay out the pattern on the ground to make sure the spacing will fit your pattern.

3 Remove all vegetation and excavate the ground to the depth of the railway sleepers.

4 Place the railway-sleeper edgings in position, setting them lengthwise to the two string lines.

5 Using a circular saw, cut the remaining railway sleepers to fit across the path. Place these cross sleepers in position to create bays to take five brick widths. The sleepers

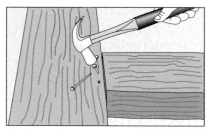

5 Place the cross sleepers in position to create the bays. Fix them together by skewing nails across the joint.

7 Pack the sand firmly in the bays and level off the excess using the screed board.

This combination of brick and railway sleepers looks well in an informal garden, but bear in mind that building such dual-material pathways requires more time spent in organisation and construction.

have butt or square joints, fixed together by skewing 75 mm lost-head nails across the joint. Use three nails per joint to hold the sleeper framework together. Pre-drill the holes to prevent the wood from splitting. Using a spirit level, check the surface is level.

6 Prepare a notched screed board (see step 6 of the Cobbled path, page 128), making the notch 8–10 mm less than the brick thickness to allow for later compaction.

7 Fill the bays with sufficient coarse-grained bedding sand for screeding.

Brick and concrete are also good choices when it comes to planning a combination path. Here old bricks are laid around concrete slabs, and the path is edged by bricks placed on their side.

SELECTING MATERIALS

Combination paths provide a meeting place for various elements in the landscape, where aspects such as texture and colour can be contrasted or blended.

Before selecting your materials, decide whether you want harmony or contrast in the finished path. Harmonious combinations have similar colours and are of similar material origin, such as timber stepping stones and bark chip, or bricks and gravel. Contrasting combinations can be based on colour or choice of materials, such as a white pebbled path edged with red bricks, or brick paving with timber, used as a dividing header and edging.

When selecting materials for a combined path, limit your choice to only two or three to avoid a piecemeal appearance.

Pack the sand firmly and screed off the excess. This path is screeded using the raised rail method (for details, see page 80).

ADDING THE BRICKS

8 Lay the bricks in a stretcher pattern (if preferred, other patterns can be used). Lay the whole bricks first, and cut the half bricks. A club hammer and bolster will easily cut house bricks.

9 Firm the bricks down. A club hammer and timber straight-edge are sufficient for compacting the bricks for this path. The straight-edge should be long enough to cover the width of the path. Move the straight-edge down the path, hitting along the top of the wood with the hammer. As the bricks are held in place by the timber edging, there is no need to hold the edge bricks in place during this process.

10 Grout the bricks with fine sand or a dry mortar mix (of 6 parts sand to 1 part cement). Use a stiff-bristled broom to sweep the sand or mix into the joints. Sweep away the excess, and finish by hosing off with a fine spray of water).

11 To build the single sleeper step, refer to pages 116–18.

8 Lay the bricks in a stretcher pattern. Fill the bays with the whole bricks first.

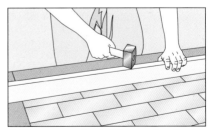

9 To ensure the bricks are level with the timber, compact them using a club hammer and straight-edge.

Cobbled path

Cobbles are large, round stones or shingles that are found on beaches and in rivers. Cobbled paths can be straight or curved, since the loose material needs only to be stabilised and contained within formwork.

METHOD

1 Make the initial preparations and lay out the path following the instructions given on pages 74–80. Set the string lines to the finished height and spacing for the path. The path in this project is 1.2 m wide.

2 Excavate and remove all vegetation to a depth of 100 mm below the finished height of the path.

3 Using 100 x 38 mm treated pine, form up the rails to be used as timber edges for the cobble path. Set the timber edges to the finished string line height.

4 Cut the 100 x 38 mm pointed pegs and hammer them into the ground on the outside of the rails every 1.2 m. Fix the timber pegs to the nails using 50 mm nails. The pegs should be approximately 300–450mm long, depending on the soil type. The finished height of the peg is approximately two-thirds of the finished height of the rail.

5 Re-seal any cut surfaces on the rail or pegs with preservative to ensure protection from ground contact.

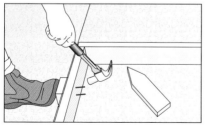

4 Fix pegs on the outside of the rails, spacing them 1.2 m apart. The pegs will support the timber edges.

6 This path is screeded using the raised rail method (see Screeding, page 80). Cut a notched screed board

Cobbles have excellent drainage and drying qualities, and they provide a wonderful contrast and colour emphasis within the garden. Gardens with an oriental influence often feature cobbled paths in their formal designs.

from a piece of timber that is wider than the path. Cut notches in both ends so that the screed board sits inside the edging rails to a depth of 50 mm.

7 Mix up a dry mortar mix of fine-grained sand and cement in a ratio of 3:1. Spread the dry mortar mix between the rails, 50 mm deep.

> HINT
>
> Cobbled paths have a rustic appearance, but they can have a very uneven surface which can be uncomfortable to walk on. To make the path easier to walk along, consider placing stepping stones along the middle of the path, within the cobbles.

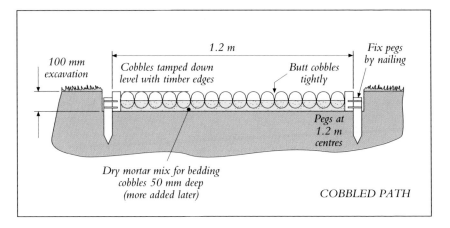

100 mm excavation

1.2 m

Cobbles tamped down level with timber edges

Butt cobbles tightly

Fix pegs by nailing

Pegs at 1.2 m centres

Dry mortar mix for bedding cobbles 50 mm deep (more added later)

COBBLED PATH

8 Pull the screed board over the rails to level the surface.

9 Position the cobbles tightly together on the surface of the dry mortar mix.

10 Use a timber straight-edge and a club hammer to tap the cobbles and press them firmly and evenly into the dry mortar mix. The cobbles should be recessed into the mix to at least half their depth.

11 Add more dry mortar mix to the surface of the path so the level is as close to the finished height of the

cobbles as possible. Remember, when you add water to the dry mix, the finished height will drop. Use a broom to sweep the mix into the spaces between the cobbles.

12 Set the hose nozzle on a fine spray and moisten the entire path with water. This will wash the cobbles clean and soak the dry mortar mix so that it will set firmly, holding the cobbles in place.

13 Allow the mortar to dry and, for a smoother finish, add an extra layer. Leave this to set.

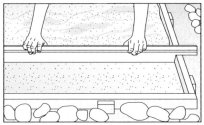

8 Using a notched screed board, pull it over the rails to level the surface of the dry mortar mix.

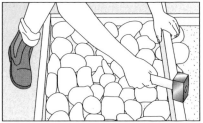

10 Using a timber straight-edge and a club hammer, tap the cobbles to press them firmly into the dry mix.

Tools for paving

Some of the most useful tools for paving are shown below. Build up your tool kit gradually – most of the tools can be purchased from your local hardware store.

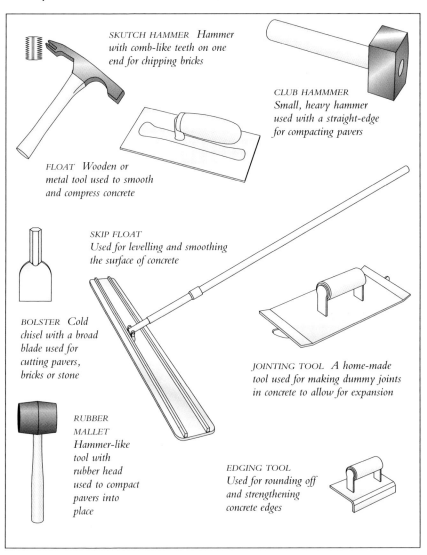

SKUTCH HAMMER *Hammer with comb-like teeth on one end for chipping bricks*

CLUB HAMMMER *Small, heavy hammer used with a straight-edge for compacting pavers*

FLOAT *Wooden or metal tool used to smooth and compress concrete*

SKIP FLOAT *Used for levelling and smoothing the surface of concrete*

BOLSTER *Cold chisel with a broad blade used for cutting pavers, bricks or stone*

JOINTING TOOL *A home-made tool used for making dummy joints in concrete to allow for expansion*

RUBBER MALLET *Hammer-like tool with rubber head used to compact pavers into place*

EDGING TOOL *Used for rounding off and strengthening concrete edges*

Tiling

Ceramic wall tiles are available in an inexhaustible range of colours and designs and it is possible to find ones that co-ordinate perfectly with kitchen cabinets and surfaces.

Choosing tiles

Tiled surfaces are enjoying a renaissance in building and home renovations. The reasons are not surprising – tiles are not only functional but also their large range in design, colour and material makes them especially suitable for all styles of decorating.

ADVANTAGES OF TILING
Tiles have several advantages over other decorative finishes for walls or floors.

• Most types are easy to put up or to lay, especially when it comes to cutting to fit around obstructions.

• Because of the wide variety of colours, textures, patterns and styles (even within one material), you can create your own individual designs by 'mixing and matching'.

• If a localised area becomes damaged or discoloured, it is much easier to replace one or more tiles than to 'patch' a continuous material.

CHOOSING TILES
Modern tiles are available in a larger range of materials and designs than ever before.

Basically, tiles for walls and floors divide into two groups: rigid and flexible.

Wall tiles The main rigid material here is ceramic (glazed baked clay), which comes in a huge variety of sizes, styles and designs and provides a durable, easy-to-clean surface for walls in kitchens, bathrooms and utility rooms, but may not be out of place in other rooms as decorative friezes.

The other main rigid materials used on walls are brick – thin brick (or stone) effect tiles stuck on to the wall surface (e.g. around a fireplace) – and mirror tiles, stuck in place with small adhesive tabs in place of a whole large mirror. Flexible wall tiles are mostly cork, which are glued in place.

Floor tiles If you are using rigid ceramic tiles for a floor, you need to be sure that they are the slip-resistant type; never use ceramic wall tiles on floors as they are too thin. Ceramic floor tiles can be bought in a wide variety of colours and designs, including those that imitate slate, marble, granite and terrazzo – though all these materials are available in their own right as tiles for use in flooring.

There is a good range of flexible floor tiling, which has the advantage that it is quieter and warmer underfoot than rigid floor tiling. Cork, carpet, vinyl and lino tiles are the most common, but you may also be able to get rubber tiles for use in the home.

CERAMIC TILES

Ceramics are the most popular tiles currently used. They are not restricted to bathrooms and utility rooms, but are used in kitchens, entrances, dining rooms, lounges, and even in

bedrooms. On a large floor expanse they impart a feeling of elegance and timelessness. A bathroom that features well-laid ceramic tiles on walls and floors has a look of quality.

Ceramic tiles can help conserve energy, especially in houses designed using sound solar principles. If the tiles are laid directly on concrete slab floors, the winter sun will heat both the tiling and concrete, keeping the home warmer. During summer, if the surface is shaded from the sun by large eaves or awnings, the tiles and slab remain cool, effectively keeping the home cool.

Ceramic tiles are available in a large range of styles, types and finishes. Types include:

• traditional soft biscuit and glazed tiles;

• unglazed tiles (mainly for floors);
• tessellated and other period tiles for heritage and period restorations.

The majority of ceramic wall tiles are square – either around 10 cm or 15 cm though other shapes and sizes are available. Floor tiles are generally larger – typically 30 cm square.

Because ceramic tiles expand slightly, lay them with a grout joint of 2–6 mm. The expansion will occur in the first few years and is a feature of any kiln-fired material. The grout compresses to accommodate this minute expansion.

Many ceramic tiles are imported – often individual shops import their own exclusive range of tiles, available nowhere else, so when buying tiles ensure you purchase sufficient amounts to allow for wastage or check they have large quantities in stock. Always buy ceramic tiles from

reputable tiling shops staffed by knowledgeable staff. They will help with tile selection, choice of adhesive systems, preparation of surfaces and be able to give you hints on how to best tackle the tiling job.

TERRACOTTA TILES

Terracotta tiles are a fired-clay tile and give a warm, earthy glow in many applications. Terracotta tiles are suited for both interior and exterior use and are laid in the same way as ceramic tiles.

Terracotta tiles are somewhat softer and more porous than ceramic tiles and for this reason they are commonly sealed when used inside the home. Suppliers of the tiles will provide suitable sealers and give advice on maintenance. If used outside where they will absorb moisture, the tiles are best left uncoated as salts would be trapped under the sealers, resulting in a poor appearance. Ceramic tiles are now made to simulate terracotta but they are much harder and less porous.

QUARRY AND PAVING TILES

Quarry and paving tiles come and go in popularity. They can be dimensionally fairly inaccurate, quite thick and have prominent ribs on the reverse side. They are always laid in a thick bed of adhesive with a wide grout joint of 12 mm or more to allow for the dimensional variation.

These tiles are very durable and usually have a rough surface to make them suited for use in areas exposed to the weather.

NATURAL STONE TILES

In the last few years, natural stone tiles such as slate, marble and granite have become more affordable. Most take a high polish, are durable and easy to care for. As marble and granite tiles are a prestige product, most home owners have them installed by a professional tiler experienced in these materials. These tiles are not fired and can be laid with minimal grouting joints.

SLATE

Slate is a metamorphic rock with a laminated structure. Like ceramic tiles, slate tiles are rigid and require a solid base although special adhesives are available for laying slate on timber floors. Slate does not tend to crack as much as ceramic tiles because of its laminated structure, but it can become loose if there is no allowance for movement.

Slate tiles are not always easy to clean because of their irregular surface. When slate is used indoors it is normally sealed to highlight its colours, lift its appearance and repel moisture and stains. Regular recoating is necessary as the surface scuffs and wears.

MARBLE

Marble is generally limited to bathrooms, although some more stately homes have marble entrances and formal rooms. Polished marble is easily scratched by sand, so an intermediate area between outdoors and a marble floor is desirable to allow feet to drop their abrasive load before reaching the marble. Marble can also stain and lose its polish if exposed to acidic materials such as wine and vinegar, making it a poor choice for kitchens.

GRANITE

Granite is nearly indestructible as it is very hard and has great abrasion resistance. It is polished in tiles similar to marble and can be used anywhere. It also needs minimal grouting joints.

VINYL AND CORK TILES

Unlike ceramic tiles which are hard and rigid, resilient floor coverings such as vinyl and cork are softer underfoot, making them a popular choice in kitchens and family rooms.

VINYL TILES

Vinyl tiles are quite durable if correctly installed on a suitable underlay. They wear well and need little maintenance but if installed on floor boards without an underlay, the imprint of the flooring timber will become visible and lead to cracking.

Only install vinyl tiles on timber floors that are well ventilated and dry, or concrete floors that have thoroughly dried after proper curing. Concrete floors must be at least three months old prior to tiling with vinyl. Vinyl is impervious to moisture and can trap water, causing moisture bubbles to for – this can cause damage to timber floors. When buying vinyl tiles check to make sure that all the packages have the same batch number to avoid colour differences.

CORK TILES

Cork tiles are another resilient floor covering and are available either polyurethane coated or unfinished. Cork is available in a range of thicknesses from 3 to 8 mm. The thin tiles are for walls and light floor use only. Use the

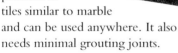

Ceramic floor tiles are a good choice for wet areas such as a bathroom, and because they have a durable, hard surface they can withstand vigorous cleaning.

thicker tiles for a kitchen or any heavy traffic area. Cork is laid on an underlay. Precoated cork is suitable for non-wet areas such as family rooms and dining areas. In the kitchen or bathroom, use unfinished tiles and apply three or four coats of polyurethane varnish to form a seamless water-resistant finish.

If the underfloor area is damp, the impervious polyurethane finish will bubble rather than allow moisture through. Cork floors can take quite an amount of abuse but sharp chair and table legs will gouge the floor deeply and be difficult to sand out. General wear of the polyurethane finish is normal and you will need to recoat the floor every five to ten years.

CARPET TILES

Carpet tiles can be used anywhere you might use normal carpet, but have the big advantage that they can be individually replaced if they get damaged. With a rubber backing, they are 50 cm square, but can easily be cut down or into shapes.

Ceramic tile basics

Whether you are tiling a floor or wall, you will need certain basic skills. These include cutting and sawing tiles, allowing provision for tile expansion and sealing tiles to other materials.

CUTTING CERAMIC TILES

1 Ceramic tiles are not very difficult to cut, but always select cutting equipment that is suited to the size of the project. Most wall tiles can be cut by scoring and snapping down. To determine where to cut a tile to fill a gap with square corners, place the front of the tile over the last free tile. Line it up, allowing for a grouting gap and a small expansion gap of 6 mm. Use a pencil to mark the edge of the tile at the cutting point and then transfer the marks to the face of the tile.

2 Using the tile scorer, score along the marked line.

3 Place a match or nail under the scored line on the tile and snap down to break the tile.

CUTTING TILES – ALTERNATIVE METHOD

Try this alternative method for cutting tiles, especially if the area to be tiled is not square:

1 Hold a full tile over the last full tile in a row.

2 Place a second tile over the first and slide it to the wall, allowing for grouting and expansion gaps.

3 Run a pencil line on to the bottom tile along the edge of the top tile to indicate where the tile is to be cut.

4 Score along the marked line and snap over a match or nail.

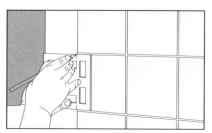

1 Place the tile face side to the wall and mark on the edge where the tile is to be cut.

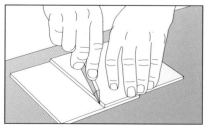

2 Use a tile scorer to score along the pencil line marked on the front of the tile.

When full tiles are not needed, use the scoring and snapping method to cut them. Tile pincers can be used to nibble into the tile so that it will fit around awkward shapes.

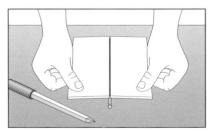

3 Place a match or nail under the tile, aligning it with the scored line, and snap the tile.

TILE SNAPPERS

Tile snappers look a bit like a large pair of pliers but are used to break scored tiles in place of the snapping method described left. After the tile has been scored, the jaws of the snappers are aligned with the score mark and the handles squeezed, giving a clean break. Some tile snappers have an in-built scorer.

CUTTING MACHINES

On a large project, or when using quarry or terracotta tiles which are extremely hard and will not necessarily snap along the scored line, hiring a tile cutting machine is a good option. The tile is placed on a central bar of the machine, a wheel attached to the lever scores the tile, and the lever is then pressed down to crack the tile along the mark. This machine gives much better leverage and control, especially when dealing with hard and large tiles.

For really hard tiles – quarry and terracotta, for example – you can hire either an angle grinder or a bench tile saw with a diamond cutting wheel to make cutting easier.

CUTTING SHAPES

An L-shape is common in wall tiles (to fit round electric socket outlets or window reveals in a kitchen, for example). One half of the L can be cut using a tile saw (see below) and the other half using the scoring and snapping method described before. Tile saws can also be used for cutting curved shapes (to fit round window sills) and holes.

SAWS FOR TILES

If you own an electric jigsaw, you can buy special tungsten-carbide coated blades which are used for cutting through ceramic and other hard tiles. The saw needs to be used on a low speed, but both straight lines and gentle curves can be cut quickly and easily.

The alternative is a tile saw – a thin tungsten carbide-coated rod-like blade held in a saw frame a bit like a coping saw. This can be used for cutting straight lines and both tight and gentle curves, but needs to be used gently to prevent the blade breaking. The blade can be replaced.

FINISHING OFF

Once the tile is cut and if the edges are rough, smooth them with a carborundum sharpening stone. Alternatively, use a tile file to smooth off any rough edges.

CUTTING HOLES

If you need to cut a hole in a tile (for example, to fit around a pipe), the first thing to do is to mark the tile out carefully, taking measurements from the surrounding tiles to mark the position of the hole exactly. Since the tile will have to be fitted in two halves, mark a line through the centre of the hole and score and snap along this line.

You now have to remove the two semicircles. This can be done either by using a tile saw (or jigsaw fitted with a ceramic tile cutting blade) or by carefully removing the waste bit by bit, using tile 'nibblers'. In either case the rough edge will need to be smoothed with a tile file or carborundum stone.

EXPANSION AND CONTROL JOINTS FOR CERAMIC TILES

Ceramic tiles, and for that matter, all fire clay products including bricks, expand slightly with age as the tile absorbs moisture to reach equilibrium with its environment. This is a slow process that may take several years. The expansion in a single tile is minuscule, but when added together over a large area it can make a substantial difference. Grouting joints take up some of this expansion if the tiles do not touch each other when laid and if the grout is compressible. When planning your tiling project, you must allow for this expansion to avoid the tiles popping off the floor or wall.

Where grout (here coloured) is used between tiles and other surfaces, frequent replacement may be needed.

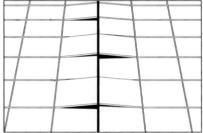

Allow for tile expansion to avoid the tiles popping off the wall or floor.

JOINING CERAMIC TILES TO OTHER MATERIALS

Wherever ceramic tiling joins a dissimilar surface such as laminate, porcelain, steel or timber, there may be some differential movement between the materials. Over time, grout may crack and need replacing

frequently. To prevent this, use a flexible silicone sealant.

TILING AROUND BATHS, BASINS AND SHOWER TRAYS

Water will leak behind a bath, basin or shower tray where the tiling joins the top rim unless it is well sealed. Again the best type of sealant to use is a flexible silicone one which allows for movement – particularly of plastic baths and shower trays. Ordinary tiling grout will crack.

Some shower trays have an upturned lip to fit behind the bottom row of tiles, which helps prevent leaks through any failed sealant.

A shower is a tiling challenge, but with care can provide a completely waterproof and good-looking result. This one has a preformed and prefinished shower tray.

Tiling a shower

Installing a shower is a very popular home improvement. A major part of the job will be tiling the enclosure and getting a good seal between the tiles and the shower tray.

PREPARATION
Before tiling, all the plumbing (and electrical) work to install the shower needs to be carried out and the shower tray put in place.

The shower tray may need to be mounted on a plinth to get the necessary drainage fall. Prepare the walls (and the plinth next to the shower tray) as for Tiling a wall, page 171.

ADHESIVES
Always use waterproof tile adhesive (and grout) when tiling a shower.

SETTING OUT
1 Decide where the cut tiles are going to go – for this project they have been put at the bottom, where they will be less obvious.

2 With a concealed shower (where all the pipework is hidden), positioning of the shower valve and shower head is vital to minimise tile cutting. Here, both are at the junction of four tiles.

FIXING THE TILES
3 Set out the position of the tiles on the walls (see Tiling a wall, page 173) and fix battens below the lowest full row of tiles.

4 Tile the walls as for a normal wall, cutting the tiles to go round the shower valve and shower head.

5 At the corners, take the tiles on one wall right into the corner (with no grouting gap) and then overlap the edges of these tiles with the tiles on the adjacent wall – this time leaving a gap for grouting.

6 When all the full tiles are laid, remove the batten and fit the edge tiles and, finally, the plinth tiles.

7 Grout as for wall tiles (page 176), paying particular attention to corners.

8 When the grout has dried, apply silicone sealant all around the shower tray in a colour to match the tile grout – usually white.

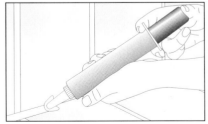

8 Apply silicone sealant around the shower tray for a waterproof join between the tray and the tiles.

Tiling a floor with ceramic tiles 1

It is easy to lay ceramic tiles on a floor. All you need is good planning, some basic skills, patience and a few inexpensive tools. When tiling a floor you have the luxury of being able to 'dry tile' the area first to see how it will look before fixing the tiles permanently in place with adhesive.

TILING WET AREAS

When tiling a 'wet' room such as a bathroom with both floor and wall tiles, tile the floor first so that the wall tiles overlap the floor tiles. This will help the water to run off. Professional tilers usually do the walls first so they can tile both surfaces in one day. You will not be that fast.

TILE QUANTITIES

If you buy tiles by the box, the coverage (in square metres) will be stated on the box. One way of estimating is to measure the length and width of the area to be covered and then to increase the dimension to make it a multiple of full tile sizes. For example, if the room measures 2.5 x 3.8 m and you are laying 30 cm square tiles, increase the room measurements to 2.7 x 3.9 m. This gives an allowance for cutting full tiles and wastage. Multiply the measurements to give you the area in square metres. If there are irregular alcoves or if the room being tiled is L-shaped, work out the area of the largest space and add to this the area of the minor floor space or spaces. Likewise, if there are projections into the floor or other areas that are not to be tiled, subtract their area from the total (see diagram, page 148).

If you are using feature tiles, order them by the quantity needed and make an allowance in the total area for these extra tiles. Where you want to tile a floor in an intricate pattern using several colours, draw a scale pattern of the floor and colour it in. Calculate the numbers of the various tiles needed and order the tiles by the number needed. This pattern sheet will be invaluable when you do the actual layout on the floor.

If you buy the tiles singly, work out the area as before, divide it by the area of a single tile and add 5 per cent for wastage and cutting (10 per cent for small tiles or if the shop will take back unused tiles).

A simple way of working out how many tiles you need is to make up a 'gauging' stick (a timber batten marked off in tile sizes plus grouting gaps), which will show at a glance how many tiles are needed each way.

The different elements in this bathroom are held together by colour. The feature tiles used for the border on the wall not only break up expanses of the one colour but also bring out the warmth of the terracotta coloured floor tiles.

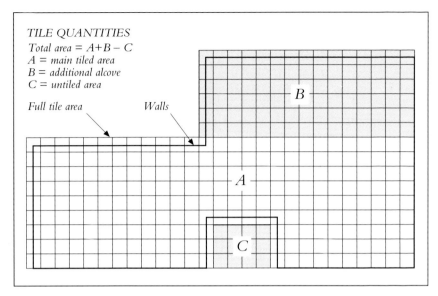

TILE QUANTITIES
Total area = A+B − C
A = main tiled area
B = additional alcove
C = untiled area

Full tile area   Walls

PREPARATION OF FLOOR SURFACES

Ensure that the floor is completely clean and if it has been previously painted or varnished remove at least 75 per cent of the paint by coarse sanding or scraping. Always lay tiles on a firm base. Tiles are completely rigid and, if laid on a non-rigid surface, the bond between the existing floor and the tile is likely to break.

The ideal surface on which to lay ceramic floor tiles is a concrete floor. In the UK, this will usually be a downstairs room (most upstairs floors are floorboards or chipboard sheet flooring) and will normally be completely flat. If it is a 'wet' bathroom (with a central waste), remember that the floor must slope downwards towards the waste so that water can run away.

Suspended timber floors covered with floorboards will normally need some additional kind of covering once the condition of the floorboards has been made good.

Take up any old vinyl, linoleum or cork floor coverings and remove as much of the old adhesive as possible. For best results, resurface a timber floor by sanding it. Use a special flexible tile adhesive if there are adhesive residues from old vinyl floors.

CONCRETE FLOORS
Concrete is a straightforward surface to tile. It must be clean and at least four weeks old. The ideal finish is a 'wood float finish' which means it has a slightly sandy texture.

Top the floor with a 1:3 cement/sand mix using a bonding agent to give the topping good adhesion to the existing floor. This gives you the opportunity to provide the necessary 'fall' if the room has a central waste.

Existing concrete floors must be dry and level. If there are just slight signs of damp, it is usually possible to 'paint' on a damp-proofing compound, which will prevent the damp going any further; if the damp is serious, the floor will have to be taken up and re-laid, incorporating a damp-proof membrane.

What is more likely is that an existing concrete floor will have cracks and hollows (both easily repaired using a sand/cement mix) or that it is not level – something which can be remedied by use of a floor-levelling compound. First, clean the floor thoroughly. Next, tip the floor-levelling compound out on to the uneven floor and trowel it smooth.

Self-levelling floor compound will fill holes of up to 5 mm, but you will need to remove (and replace) skirting boards and you may need to trim the bottom off doors opening into the room to allow for the thickness of the compound and the new tiled floor covering.

TIMBER FLOORS

An existing chipboard sheet floor should not pose too many problems – which is just as well, because getting individual tongued-and-grooved sheets up is not easy!

The main point to watch here is whether 'inspection hatches' have been left in the flooring to allow access to underfloor pipes and electric wiring. If they have, you will have to match these hatches in any covering (including the tiling) which you put on top, so that future access is still possible.

Floorboards are much more likely to need attention before you can lay a ceramic tiled floor covering on top. This is especially true when laying something like cork tiles since any imperfections in the underlying floor show clearly through the cork, in contrast to ceramic tiles which have the thickness of adhesive to take up the odd ripple.

The first thing is to replace any floorboards which are damaged (split, cracked or rotten) and to hammer home any protruding nails. If the floorboards are loose, replace the nails with screws. If the floor is still uneven – a common fault is 'cupping' of the boards, where they lift up at the edges – hire an industrial floor sander to bring the floorboards back to a smooth and level surface, but make sure there are no protruding nails first.

Before laying ceramic tiles on a timber floor, you should put down an underlay. If you are certain that the basic floor is level (sanded floorboards or chipboard sheet flooring), sheets of hardboard nailed in place should be sufficient; if there is any unevenness, you can either use the kind of sand/cement 'screed' used on solid floors or lay 6 mm plywood nailed or screwed down in place.

EXISTING TILES

Existing tiles – whether on walls or floors – are in many ways the ideal surface on which to lay new tiles, since the preparation work will have been done before and the surface will be – or should be – perfectly flat. On a floor, you will need to think about the consequences of the extra thickness, which could mean trimming the bottom of doors.

Check that every tile is sound and well adhered. Loosely run the handle of a large screwdriver over every floor tile. You will hear a hollow, 'drummy' sound when a loose tile is encountered. Remove and replace any loose tiles (see box on Tiling problems, opposite). Alternatively, fill the spaces left with a mixture of 1:3 of cement and sand together with a bonding agent and allow it to dry.

For information on Replacing cracked tiles, refer to page 159.

FLOOR WASTES

Wastes or drainage are required in bathroom and utility room floors in case water accidentally overflows. No water should stand on the tiled floor. Make an appropriate fall with a cement topping or allow for the fall when laying the tile adhesive.

When laying large tiles, wherever possible, align the tiles so that four tiles meet at the floor waste. This makes cutting the tiles around the waste and getting the correct fall much easier. For details of how to cut curves in tiles, see page 142.

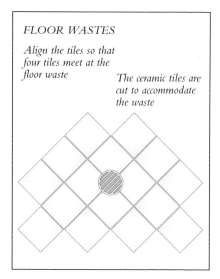

FLOOR WASTES

Align the tiles so that four tiles meet at the floor waste

The ceramic tiles are cut to accommodate the waste

ADHESIVES AND MORTARS

Whether you use a traditional mortar or a modern floor tiling adhesive depends on the base substrate, the type of tile and the cost.

● Conventional sand/cement mixes are economical but difficult for the amateur to use. As the consistency of mix and timing is critical, bonding agents are added to increase the adhesive properties.

● Prepared cement-based floor tiling adhesives are more expensive but easy to use. They are ideal for natural (slate or stone) tiles or man-made (rather than machine-made) quarry tiles where thicknesses may vary.

● Special adhesives are available for floors which may experience periodic movement, such as timber floors.

● Most adhesive manufacturers have a technical department that can give you advice regarding your particular project or if something is not clear.

TILING PROBLEMS

CRACKED GROUT

It is not unusual for grout between tiles to crack or erode because of vigorous cleaning. Cracks can be a sign of movement in the building or be related to tile expansion. Regardless of the cause, the repair to the grout is simple.

Rake out as much of the old grout as possible using a screwdriver or hardened grout raking tool. Floor grout is normally a cement mortar and difficult to remove without damaging the tiles. In this case, regrout over the top of the existing grout as if it were new tiling (see Grouting, page 155).

LOOSE TILES

Tiles which sound 'drummy' are no longer firmly adhered to the wall or floor and can spring off the surface at any time. The main causes of looseness are:
• failure of old adhesives
• incorrect tiling in the first place
• fixing the tiles too close together and not allowing for tile expansion.

Probably the biggest problem in modern tiling is the tendency to lay tiles too close together. Tiles permanently expand with age and if they are laid hard against each other in large areas they have nowhere to expand except off the wall or floor. Carefully remove loose wall tiles from the top down, placing a soft blanket on the floor to catch the tiles you cannot control. Remove the old adhesive by scraping it off as best you can and replace the tiles using a flexible, two-part adhesive.

If you have large areas of tiling without an expansion joint that have not yet failed, consider cutting a joint every 5 m following a grout joint. Hire an angle grinder to cut a slot through the joint and the adhesive bed. Fill the joint with a flexible mastic or sealant to match the colour of the grout.

If the existing tiles are cracked and need replacing see Replacing cracked tiles, page 159.

MOULD IN GROUTING

Most grout is porous and holds water. It is the ideal environment for mould spores to grow in. Clean the joints frequently with a bathroom cleaner, grout reviver or use chlorinated bleach which kills the mould for a while.

When replacing grout which has suffered from mould growth, make sure you use a 'waterproof' grout, which contains a fungicide specifically to inhibit mould.

If the mould growth is behind a silicone sealant near the shower screen or around the bath, cut away the silicone with a sharp utility knife and reseal the joint using new silicone sealant.

Tiling a floor with ceramic tiles 2

When choosing tiles for flooring projects, select tiles that are hard wearing and non-slip. Large expanses of tiling on floors can look very effective if contrasting border or feature tiles are introduced.

SETTING OUT
1 Start by setting out the tiles. This can be done in several ways:
- Quarter the room and tile to the sides. Find the centre of the floor and mark a line parallel to the most visible wall. Using a builders square, draw a second line perpendicular to this to divide the room into quarters. Lay out the tiles allowing a gap of about 3–5 mm between them to allow for grouting.

Adjust the position of the tiles to minimise the number of tile cuts needed. If the tiles must be cut, it is easier to cut a tile in half than it is to cut off a thin sliver. Adjust the two lines accordingly (see the diagram below).

TOOLS
- Tape measure
- String line and pins
- Spirit level (900 mm) and straight-edge
- Builders square (3:4:5 triangle)
- Tungsten-tipped tile scorer or tile cutting machine
- Tile pincers
- Buckets (several) for mixing prepared adhesive and water
- Spatula
- Notched trowel, with 10 or 12 mm notches (for spreading adhesive)
- Nylon spacing crosses
- Sponge or scouring pads
- Rubber squeegee (for grouting)

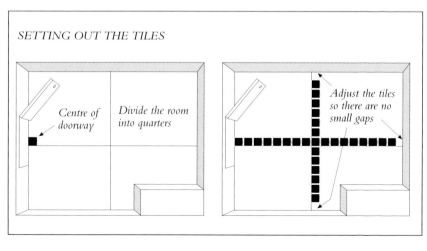

SETTING OUT THE TILES

Centre of doorway

Divide the room into quarters

Adjust the tiles so there are no small gaps

Grey and cream feature tiles work well when incorporated in this large expanse of plain tiles; the kitchen might otherwise look quite stark. The tiles are laid working on roughly one quarter of the room at a time.

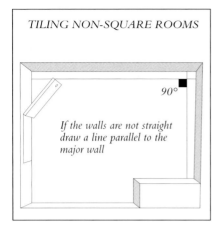

TILING NON-SQUARE ROOMS

90°

If the walls are not straight draw a line parallel to the major wall

• Establish a line of tiles in the major field of vision as you enter the room.
• If necessary, centre tiles on a prominent feature.
• Start from a prominent corner. If the corner and the walls running from the corner are actually square, the tiles can run from the corner, but first check that the tile cut at the opposite end will be easy to make.

However, do not rely on the walls or corners of a room always being straight or square. This last method can be adapted to walls that are not square by drawing a line parallel to the major wall (see the diagram above) and adjusting the tiling so that there are no small cuts needed. Remember, a gap between the wall and floor tiles is necessary to allow for tile expansion.

If the room has expansion or control joints, do not tile over them. Align your tiling along one edge of the joint, tile the other side and when the tiling is finished, fill the gap with a matching flexible sealant.

LAYING THE TILES

2 Decide where you are going to work first. Work on roughly one quarter of the room at a time, starting with the corner furthest from the door to give you an exit.

3 Load the adhesive on the floor with the spatula and spread it using the notched trowel. Find the correct size of trowel on the adhesive container – it will vary with the type of tile and flooring material. Normally a 10 mm or 12 mm trowel will be appropriate. The trowel creates ridges in the adhesive to improve the grip on the back of the tile. Hold the trowel vertically to the floor to spread and rib the adhesive. Only spread enough adhesive to cover a maximum of one square metre at a time.

4 Place the tiles in the adhesive as soon as possible and settle them in place with a twist of the hand to bed them well in. Occasionally remove a tile to make sure you are achieving an adhesive coverage of at least 80–90 per cent. Air bubbles under the tiles can cause loose tiles.

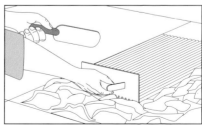

3 *Using the notched trowel held vertically to the floor, spread and rib the adhesive.*

5 If the tiles have ribs on the reverse side, 'butter' the tiles individually to ensure a complete coverage of adhesive and to prevent the ribs being in direct contact with the substrate rather than the adhesive.

6 Use nylon spacing crosses to achieve constant grout joint widths. If the tiles vary in dimension, use a stretched string line to ensure that the rows of joints are straight and even. Check tile edges are not raised as these could cause accidents.

7 Lay the bulk of full tiles in a small area before filling in the cut tiles. Remember that you will need access to back corners to install the corner tiles. Make sure you can reach or you will have to wait for the next day. If you must reach across the tiles, use a 450 x 900 mm piece of 12 mm plywood to use as a kneeling board. After using the board check that all tiles are still in correct alignment.

8 Gently clean off the excess adhesive before it sets, using a damp sponge and rinsing it frequently. If you have to interrupt your tiling, remove all excess adhesive on the floor right up to the last tile laid while it is still wet and discard it.

GROUTING

9 Leave the tiles for at least 24 hours before grouting them. For floors, the material used for grouting is usually the same mix as was used for laying. Special floor grout mixes are also available, but light coloured grout will tend to become soiled quickly. Most adhesive manufacturers suggest you add bonding agents to the grout when using them on timber floors to give extra resilience to the mix when dry. Apply grout with a rubber squeegee, working the grout well into the joints at an angle.

10 Using a soft sponge, wipe off any excess before it has time to set, rinsing the sponge frequently.

11 Once the tiles are grouted, allow a further 24 hours before polishing the surface with a soft, dry cloth or crumpled newspaper. After polishing, the floor may be used.

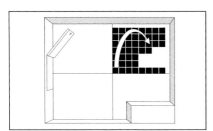

7 Lay the bulk of the tiles by tiling out from the centre of the room to the edges.

9 Use a rubber squeegee to apply the grout, working the grout well into the joints of the tiles.

Tiled floor waste

Make a bathroom or shower floor waste a feature by tiling around the waste with concentric circles of small, attractive tiles. This project will work best where the waste is in the centre of the floor. Tumbled marble tiles of standard shapes were used for this project but small ceramic tiles are also suitable.

METHOD

1 The preparation of the surface and the tiling methods and materials used to tile the floor waste are the same as for normal ceramic floor tiling (see Tiling a floor with ceramic tiles 1 and 2, pages 146–55). If you need to provide a fall to the waste, use a sand/cement screed to form it, not the tile adhesive.

2 Draw a circle measuring the diameter of the floor waste on a large sheet of hardboard or plywood and set out the tiles around it. Write down the outside radius of each circle of tiles and the number of tiles in each circle. This will be a helpful guide for when you are ready to fix the tiles in place.

3 Transfer this information to the actual floor. To draw the circles, tie a loop in a length of string and slip this over a pencil. Put the pencil in the centre of the floor waste. The other end can be wound around a second pencil and adjusted to draw the various circles.

4 Divide the room into quarters using the waste as the centre of the intersecting lines. Draw heavy black lines that can be seen once the adhesive is laid and ribbed.

5 Use a 6 mm notched trowel to apply the cement-based adhesive to the inside circle. Position the tiles according to your design. Where the number of tiles in a circle can be

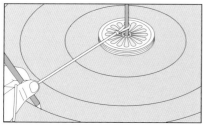

3 Transfer the measurements and use a pencil and string to draw concentric circles on the floor.

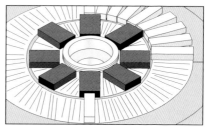

5 Where there are even numbers of tiles in a circle, align them with the lines defining room quarters.

When choosing tiles for the floor waste aim for a subtle effect rather than something too bold that will overpower the room. These tumbled marble tiles have been sealed to protect them from staining.

divided by four, place one on each of the marked lines that define the quarters and then fill in between. Work out other patterns so that the tiles are evenly spaced around the circumference of the circle.

6 Continue working outwards in concentric circles, finishing each circle before starting the next. After laying each small section, use a block of soft timber to press the tiles in place so their surfaces are all at the same level. Check the radial alignment of tiles by running a timber batten across the centre of the waste and align opposite tiles so they are parallel to the batten.

7 As you pass the fifth or sixth circle you may need to divide the job into sections and work on a quarter or half at a time if your working space is small. This will allow you to easily exit the room.

8 Allow the adhesive to set for approximately 24 hours before grouting the tiles. Plug the waste with newspaper to avoid any grout

blocking the drain. Make the grout using 1 part off-white cement, 5 parts sand and enough tiling bonding agent to make a stiff creamy paste for good flexibility, adhesion and to avoid cracking. Use the rubber squeegee to fill the grout joints (see Grouting, page 155), being careful to fill the wide, variable joints well. When cleaning the face of the tiles, take care not to cause depressions in the wide wedges close to the waste and use a light touch with the sponge to avoid smearing grout over the tile surface. You should only have a light film of grout remaining after you have cleaned the tiles. Wait a further 24 hours before polishing the grout film off the floor. If it is difficult to clean, try using a nylon kitchen scourer.

9 As the tiles used for this project are tumbled marble tiles they can look a little dull and may stain. Contact your tile supplier for a recommended tile sealer that will make the colours more lively and protect against staining.

8 Plug the waste with newspaper and use the squeegee to work the grout well into the tile joints.

> **HINT**
> When making a radial pattern, the spaces between the tiles at the centre are quite large. A normal grout would crack badly in this situation. This is why a sand/cement grout with a bonding agent instead of water is used for this project.

REPLACING CRACKED TILES

A cracked tile can easily be removed and replaced.

1 Rake out the grout around the tile to isolate it from its neighbours.

2 Put on safety goggles and chip away at the tile with a cold chisel, working from the centre of the tile towards the edge. Do not lever the tile from the edge as you will damage adjacent tiles. Chip out all the small pieces and the adhesive.

3 Fix a new tile in place by buttering adhesive to the back of the tile and adjust it so it is in line and level with the other tiles.

TILES ON PLASTERBOARD

If the cracked tile is fixed to plasterboard, you are likely to put a hole through the board when trying to remove the tile. To prevent this from occurring, run a sharp utility knife around the tile before trying to remove it so the paper face of the plasterboard will come away rather than the plaster core.

If there is only slight surface damage to the plasterboard, you can use a wall filler to repair it before fixing a new tile. But if you have made a hole, it's best to cut out the section of plasterboard and patch the hole with new plasterboard before fixing the tile.

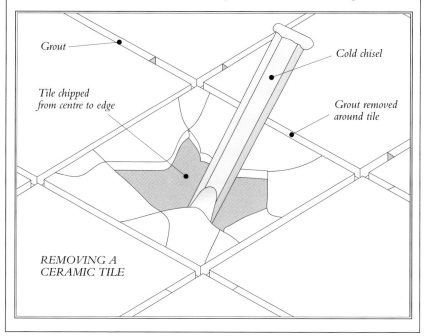

Grout

Cold chisel

Tile chipped from centre to edge

Grout removed around tile

REMOVING A CERAMIC TILE

Cork is available in a range of thicknesses – the thin tiles are inexpensive and are suitable for light use only, the thicker tiles are for use in kitchens or other heavy-traffic areas.

Tiling a floor with cork tiles

Cork is one of the most popular of the resilient floor tiles. It creates a soft, warm surface, requires little maintenance and damaged tiles can easily be replaced.

PREPARATION

Before laying down cork tiles, make sure that the surface is smooth, level and totally dust-free to achieve good adhesion and durability.

LAYING ON TIMBER

When laying cork on a timber floor ensure all nails are well nailed down and punched below the surface. The floor must be level. Hire a professional floor sander where extensive sanding is needed. All resilient floor coverings must be installed on a well-ventilated sub-floor. An underlay is needed.

LAYING ON CONCRETE

When laying cork on a concrete floor ensure the concrete is thoroughly dry. The concrete must be laid on a damp-proof membrane such as polyethylene sheet. Cork tiles are not suited to areas such as damp basement floors. In this case, ceramic tiles are the preferred covering.

It is essential that the floor is flat – if necessary, use a floor-levelling compound (see page 149).

LAYING THE UNDERLAY

Do not lay cork tiles directly on a timber strip floor as the outline of the boards will eventually show through. Lay cork on an underlay – tempered hardboard laid rough side up. Hardboard is sold in sheets approximately 1200 x 900 mm in size. Stand the sheets around the room for 24 hours before fixing to acclimatise them to the room moisture content. Loosely lay the hardboard on the floor to check the fit. Stagger the joints and don't allow the hardboard joints to coincide with flooring joints. Leave a 2 mm gap between the sheets.

On very uneven floors, use plywood sheets as an underlay for cork tiles. Nail the hardboard and smooth all joints and raised areas in the underlay with an orbital or hand sander. Thoroughly vacuum the floor. Seal the sanded areas if required by the tile adhesive manufacturer.

ADHESIVES

Some cork tiles are self-adhesive, but most need a separate adhesive.

Always use the adhesive that is recommended by the tile manufacturer – there are different types depending on the thickness of the tile and the substrate to which it is being fixed. Treat dusty floors with a recommended sealer.

TOOLS

- 3 mm notched applicator
- Adhesive
- Sanding float or orbital sander
- Paint brush or lambswool paint roller and extension
- Chalk line
- Tape
- Square pencil
- Basic carpentry tools
- Fine grade sandpaper

LAYING THE CORK

1 Set out the floor (see Tiling a floor with ceramic tiles 2, page 152).

2 Lift the tiles and apply the adhesive directly to the floor using the notched applicator. Lay a maximum of one square metre at a time. If you do more, the adhesive may form a skin and will not adhere properly to the tiles. Aim to complete at least one quarter or half of the floor area each day.

3 Align the first tile and lay it straight down without sliding it in place.

Continue laying tiles in a pyramidal pattern towards a corner.

4 When you reach a wall, cut the tiles to suit. Place a full tile over the last full tile laid in that row. Place another full tile over the first but touching the wall or skirting. Mark the lower tile and cut along this line with a sharp utility knife along a straight edge. If the cut is slightly rough, sand the edge lightly. The cut edge butts against the wall.

5 To cut a tile to fit around a corner, mark the tiles the same way on one wall and repeat on the other without rotating the tiles. Cut out the box facing the corner.

6 To fit tiles around irregularly shaped obstructions, make a cardboard template of a tile and cut 'fingers' in it to shape it around the object. Transfer to the tile and cut out. (For more complex shapes use a profile gauge.)

7 Clean any excess adhesive off the underlay as you work. Seal the floor as soon as possible to avoid staining.

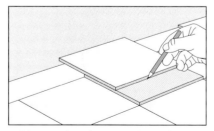

4 To cut the tiles near the wall place a tile over the last tile laid and place a third tile on top, touching the wall.

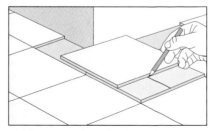

5 To cut a tile to fit around a corner, mark the tiles the same way on one wall and repeat on the other.

LAYING SELF-ADHESIVE CORK OR VINYL TILES

Self-adhesive cork or vinyl tiles are very easy to lay. Like other resilient tiles, they rely on a level, clean and totally dust-free surface.

1 Divide the floor into quarters as for ceramic tiling (see page 152) and set out the tiles to find the best spacing. It is not difficult to cut a thin strip off a tile and this gives you many spacing options.

2 Remove the backing on the first tile to expose the adhesive surface.

Place the tile in its correct position and try to avoid pushing it into position. Do not force adjacent tiles hard together; they should be placed so that they make a snug fit.

3 Cut the tiles using the overlapping method as described in step 4, page 162.

4 After laying self-adhesive vinyl floors, do not wet them for a period of at least seven days to avoid adhesion problems.

SANDING THE FLOOR

8 Tiles which are not pre-sealed will need sanding before sealing. Seal off the room by taping plastic sheeting across doorways and other openings. Wearing a mask, use an orbital sander to lightly sand the cork to smooth the surface. Try not to sand depressions into the soft cork as this is easy to do with a large powerful floor sander. Vacuum the floor when sanding is complete.

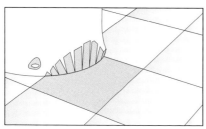

6 To fit tiles around obstructions, cut 'fingers' in a cardboard template and transfer the shape to the tile.

COATING THE FLOOR

9 The floor should now be coated with a finish (even if the tiles are pre-sealed). Some coatings use a special sealer as a first coat. If using a solvent-based finish, buy a mask with a filter for hydrocarbon fumes. Open windows to provide ventilation.

10 Apply the first coat of finish with a 50 mm paint brush around the perimeter and with a lambswool roller on an extension rod for the main part of the floor. Allow to dry then sand with fine grade sandpaper and vacuum again. Repeat this step.

11 Close the windows so dust does not settle on the third and final coat. Apply the final coat, allowing it to dry for a day before walking on the floor. Allow three or four days before subjecting the floor to light use.

Carpet tiles can give a stunning effect in a dining room when laid in a diamond pattern with colours alternating in adjacent tiles. Both the centre tile and the edge tiles have been laid with double-sided tape.

Laying carpet tiles

Carpet tiles are soft underfoot and are an excellent substitute for conventional carpet in rooms where the floor covering is likely to be damaged as they are easily replaced.

PREPARATION

Carpet tiles need a smooth, level and dust-free surface and existing floors should be prepared in the same way as for cork floors – see page 161.

ADHESIVES

Carpet tiles are usually laid 'dry' without any adhesive – which makes them particularly easy to take up for cleaning or replacement.

However, to stop the whole floor moving around, it is a good idea to stick down the centre tile or tiles and any narrow edge tiles – either with a latex-based carpet adhesive or with double-sided adhesive tape.

SETTING OUT

Carpet tiles have a pile direction (often indicated by an arrow on the back of the tile) and, when laying whole tiles, it is normal to lay adjacent tiles with the pile directions at right angles to give a slight chequerboard effect.

Whole tiles can be laid with their edges parallel to the room walls or at an angle of 45 degrees to give a diamond effect. The second method involves much more cutting of tiles – especially if you also have a straight-sided border all around the room.

LAYING THE TILES

1 Set out the floor (see Tiling a floor with ceramic tiles 2, page 152).

2 For the centre tile or tiles, stick double-side adhesive tape down on the floor, peel off the backing paper and press the tile firmly into place.

3 Work outwards from the centre of the room, butting the tiles tightly against one another, until all the whole tiles have been laid.

4 Cut the edge tiles as described for cork tiles on page 162, but cutting from the back. Lay these tiles using more double-sided adhesive tape.

5 To fit round complex shapes (e.g. architraves), transfer the shape to the tile with a profile gauge.

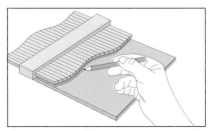

5 Use a profile gauge to transfer complex shapes to a carpet tile before cutting it.

Natural stone floors reflect natural earth colours and textures unlike any man-made tile. This also means there may be occasional blemishes or inconsistencies from one tile to the next.

Tiling with natural stone

Stone tiles, including marble, travertine, granite and quartzite, can be used as an alternative to ceramic tiles. However, the most suitable stone is natural slate which is hard wearing, non-fading and available in a range of natural, earth colours.

PREPARATION

Laying slate is very similar to laying large ceramic tiles. Like tiles, slate is often sold by area. Multiply the length and width of the area to be tiled to give you the number of square metres required. If there are areas not to be tiled subtract them from the total (see Tile quantities, page 146).

Slate, again like ceramic tiles, is a completely rigid material and, if laid on a non-rigid surface, such as timber, it could loosen and be damaged (see Preparation of floor surfaces, pages 148–50).

Slates vary in thickness. Sort them into piles of similar thickness before starting. Make three or four separate, graded piles and then use each of the piles in order of thickness. If the slate is laid on a uniformly thick bed of adhesive, the floor will have a very slight fall. As an alternative, increase the thickness of the adhesive bed slightly across the floor and lay the thinnest slates where the adhesive bed is the thickest. On a patio, a fall away from the house is recommended, so start with the thickest tiles next to the wall. In a bathroom with a central waste, the variations in slate thickness can be used to advantage to achieve the fall to the floor waste.

Slates are difficult to trim with hand tools. Therefore, start laying them against a wall or an outside edge of a patio rather than from the centre of an area. Square the rest of the project from the starter row.

Lay out the tiles and check that cuts required at the ends of rows leave pieces that are greater than 50 mm wide: small slate pieces are quite brittle and difficult to fix.

TOOLS

- Tape measure
- String line and pins
- Spirit level (900 mm) and straight-edge
- Builders square
- Buckets (several) for mixing prepared adhesive and water
- Spatula
- Notched trowel with 12 mm notches
- Sponge or scouring pads
- Diamond-bladed wet saw
- Brush and roller
- Bristle brush
- Rubber squeegee (for grouting)

Draw a line for each tile row, measuring from the starting row, and set up a string line as a guide. This avoids you making a fan-shaped pattern as small errors compound.

ADHESIVE AND MORTARS

Lay slate in either a traditional mortar or a modern adhesive. It is easiest, though more expensive, to use a proprietary adhesive and to follow the manufacturer's instructions. The traditional mortar is best left to professionals. The adhesives are cement based with workability aids and bonding agents added to give you a reasonable working time. Slate adhesives are water mixable and washable while wet. They are similar to ceramic adhesives and some manufacturers claim their adhesives are suited to both tiles and slate.

Major adhesive manufacturers have a range of special compounds specifically formulated for laying slate and ceramics on timber floors. They allow for the movement in timber floors. Others have developed special underlay systems with slip joints to allow for differential movement.

CUTTING SLATE

Hire a diamond-bladed bench tile saw or an angle grinder to cut the slate. If you try to score and snap it, the slate will split along its laminations, and not along the score mark. Bench tile saws use a diamond-tipped blade that is kept wet and cool. It is easy to use. Mark out the tiles the same way as for ceramic tiling.

Some slate tiles are supplied with a rough guillotined edge. When cutting these, make sure the cut edge is placed against the wall to avoid mismatching of the edges.

LAYING THE SLATE

1 Once the design and layout have been finalised, mix the tile adhesive according to the manufacturer's instructions. Only mix enough adhesive for about one to two square metres at a time and finish this amount of tiling before mixing more tile adhesive.

2 Spread the tile adhesive over the first square metre you intend to tile and rib the adhesive using a 12 mm notched trowel.

3 Place the tile in the correct position and gently rock it into position. Manoeuvre the slate from the centre and gently rock it back and forward to expel most of the air from underneath. Adjust the position of the tile with the wooden handle of a hammer, tapping it only near the centre. While adjusting the tile, place your other hand on it to act as a

> HINT
>
> Slates are commonly bowed and should be laid with the bow up. If they are laid the other way up, it is difficult to provide a strong enough edge bearing for the tile and it will come loose within a short time.

'shock absorber' and prevent the tile rocking back to its original position.

4 Do not butt slates up hard against each other. Leave a 6–10 mm grouting gap to allow for any slight movement in either the slate or the surface on which it is laid. This also allows for irregularities in tile size.

5 Once about a square metre of tiles has been laid, clean off any excess adhesive with a damp sponge before it sets and hardens on the surface. As you work, remove as much excess adhesive as possible with frequent changes of water. Remove the adhesive residue with a scouring pad at the end of each day. Carefully clean out any adhesive caught in the irregularities in the slate surface using a soft bristle brush. If your tiling is interrupted at any stage, clean any adhesive off the substrate so that you have a flat, clean surface when you are ready to start laying the slate again.

GROUTING AND FINISHING
6 Leave the slate for at least 24 hours before grouting. Use a rubber squeegee and the same adhesive mix as was used for laying the slate. Try to avoid working the grout into natural lamination cracks.

7 When you finish a section thoroughly clean the surface with a damp sponge and the bristle brush to clean out crevices. Allow a further 24 hours before walking on the floor.

When slate is used indoors on a floor it is sealed to highlight its colour and to repel any accidental spills.

SEALING
8 Colourful slates are usually sealed in interior locations. In external areas where moisture rises from the ground, slates are best left untreated. While there is any moisture in the slate or in the adhesive, premature sealing leads to efflorescence or white salt stains. Slate can take up to several weeks to thoroughly dry out. If there is any chance of moisture penetrating from under the slates, such as when they are laid in damp areas like the basement, leave them unsealed.

9 An acrylic sealer is the preferred finish for slate floors. Make sure the product you use is specifically designed for use on slates. Refer to the directions on the manufacturer's container for recoating times and any other special requirements. Highly coloured slates which derive their colour from the weathering bands must be thoroughly brushed off prior to coating with the sealer.

Feature tiles break up the expanse of plain white tiling on this bathroom wall.

Tiling a wall 1

In many ways, tiling walls is easier than tiling floors. The procedures for tiling a wall are the same for all rooms but more attention to waterproofing is needed in the bathroom and kitchen.

TILE QUANTITIES

Most wall tiles are square, in one of two sizes – around 10 cm or 15 cm. When you have selected the size you want, make up a gauging stick from a length of timber batten around 1.2 m long, marked out with exact tile widths and 2 mm grouting gaps. If you are not sure which size of tile to use, you could mark the batten with different sizes to see which one fits best. The gauging stick will not only enable you to work out you how many tiles you need in each direction, but it will also help you to position the tiles. As with floor tiles, cutting should be kept to a minimum (and no tile should be less than half a tile's width), but you may want to align the tiles with other features such as a bathroom basin, a kitchen sink or a window.

PREPARING THE SURFACE

You can tile most wall surfaces as long as they are dry, flat and sound. House walls are normally plaster or plasterboard, but you may find cement render or even bare brick walls.

PLASTER AND PLASTERBOARD

New plaster should be left for at least a month to dry out thoroughly before tiling. Check that there are no hollows or other blemishes which still need filling.

Old bare plaster is an ideal surface for tiling (provided it is firm), but you will need to fill cracks and holes, smoothing down the filler before putting up the tiles.

Tiles can be put directly on to plasterboard but, in many houses, the plasterboard will have already been given a skim coat of plaster.

CEMENT RENDERED SURFACES

Cement render is a good substrate for tiling and should have a sand textured 'wood float finish'. Patch any irregularities to make a flat surface. Render brick and existing smooth concrete walls before tiling.

PREVIOUSLY TILED SURFACES

Check that all tiles are sound and replace any loose or broken tiles (see Tiling problems, page 151). Thoroughly clean old tiles and remove any loose grout. Do not regrout the narrow grooves between the tiles as adhesive worked into them will help 'key' the new tiles.

DECORATED SURFACES

Sound gloss or emulsion paint can take ceramic tiles, but any loose or flaky paint should be sanded off and the whole surface cleaned thoroughly. Fill cracks and holes as for plaster. Do not attempt to tile over old distemper or a textured wall coating. Strip these off before starting and then clean and repair the wall.

You cannot tile over wallpaper, which will need to be completely stripped back to bare plaster.

ADHESIVES

Adhesives for fixing ceramic tiles to walls are available either as powders, which you mix with water, or ready-mixed in a tub (more expensive but more convenient). All-purpose adhesives can be used anywhere, but you need a waterproof adhesive where the tiling will regularly get wet – such as in shower enclosures.

Some ceramic tile adhesives can also be used for grouting; with others you will need to buy the grout (white) separately.

Glossy, smooth tiles are durable and easy to clean, making them the perfect choice for tiled areas that are likely to be splattered with cooking grease. Here white grout provides a smart contrast with the black tiles.

Tiling a wall 2

As with most tiling projects good planning is essential when tiling a wall. The important thing to remember is that the floor is not necessarily on a level plane so it is important to use a temporary batten as a starting point for the first row of tiles.

SETTING OUT

1 Think carefully about how you will set out the tiling. Start off by finding the lowest point of the floor perimeter using a spirit level. Measure and mark the wall one full tile height plus two grout joint widths from this lowest point.

2 Temporarily nail a batten to the wall with the top edge corresponding with the mark. Use a spirit level to make sure it is horizontal (the floor may not be level). If you have a rendered wall, prop the batten in place with bricks and thin packing material – this is your starting line.

3 Mark the centre of the wall on the batten and dry lay a line of tiles to see how they fit. Some tiles have spacing

TOOLS

- Batten, hammer and nails
- Spirit level and tape measure
- Straight-edge
- Plumb line
- Notched trowel (4.5 or 6 mm for flat back tiles, 10 mm for tiles with ribs)
- Buckets (several) for mixing adhesive and water
- Tile pincers
- Spatula
- Nylon spacing crosses
- Sponges or scourers
- Masking tape
- Rubber squeegee (for applying grout)
- Tile saw for cutting curves (optional)
- Tile cutter

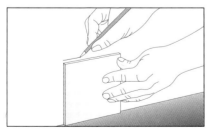

1 Find the lowest point on the floor and mark the wall one tile height plus two grout joints from the floor.

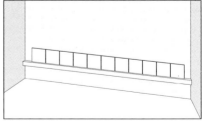

3 Set out the tiles along the batten to see how they fit. Mark their position on the batten then set them aside.

lugs to automatically give you a consistent grouting joint. Others have no spacing lugs so use nylon spacing crosses between the tiles.

4 Adjust the row of tiles so that the two end tiles will need equal cuts (see Setting out, page 152). Remember, cutting a tile in half is much easier than cutting a thin strip off a tile.

5 When you are happy with the positions of the tiles, mark them on the batten for easy reference and stack the tiles nearby, ready to lay.

6 Use a plumb line to mark a vertical line on the wall, corresponding with the end tile mark. Along this line, mark the vertical position of the tiles, especially noting the position of any feature tiles or borders. Alternatively, nail a vertical batten to the wall with its straight-edge along the last column of full tiles. The cut tiles at the corners are prepared and installed once the bulk of the tiling has been completed. Do not start tiling from a corner as it is unlikely to be perfectly square.

SETTING OUT ALTERNATIVE

If the tiling is to finish at an exact height on the wall, work down the wall in multiples of the tile size plus a 2 mm grout joint. This gives you the level at which the starting batten should be fixed. If border tiles or other patterns form part of the design, carefully work out their location on the wall.

LAYING THE TILES

7 Spread the adhesive according to the manufacturer's directions. Most wall adhesives are premixed. Apply the adhesive just above the bottom batten with a spatula or the straight edge of a trowel. Using a 4.5 mm or 6 mm notched trowel held at an angle to the wall, spread the adhesive evenly over the area to be tiled. The final pass with the notched trowel should leave uniform horizontal ribs. Tiles with ribs on the reverse side may need to be 'buttered' with adhesive to achieve good adhesion. This avoids the possibility of the ribs physically contacting the wall. Only apply enough adhesive to cover

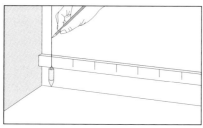

6 Use a plumb line to mark a vertical line to correspond with the end tile mark on the batten.

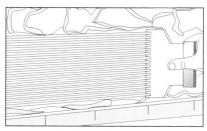

7 Spread the adhesive above the batten with a spatula then rib it horizontally with a notched trowel.

about one square metre at a time to avoid the adhesive skinning over. Do not lay tiles on adhesive that has formed a skin on the surface.

8 Start fitting the full tiles along the batten in one of the corners of the wall. All tiling beneath this batten will be either a full tile or slightly less than a full tile. You will not have to cut a thin sliver of tile as a fill in. Leave the cut tiles on the end to be fitted once all the full tiles are in place. Press the tiles firmly into the adhesive with a slight twist to ensure good coverage on the back of the tile. Occasionally remove a tile after placement to check that the adhesive coverage is at least 80–90 per cent.

9 If your tiles do not have spacing lugs, fit nylon spacers between them to give constant gaps of at least 2 mm. While nylon spacers are specifically designed for the job, matchsticks can also be used.

10 Using a spirit level, periodically check that the tiles are level both horizontally and vertically.

The setting out of the wall should include any feature or border tiles.

11 Feature, border and inset tiles are fixed to the wall at the same time as the main areas of tiling. As some feature and border tiles vary in size from standard tiles, consider carefully how you will lay them out. If this is the case, it may be better to offset the joints in the tiling rather than have the joints not quite lining up. Include some extra adhesive to the back of tile accent strips to ensure they are well bonded.

12 Remove any adhesive smears on the face of the tiles with a damp sponge. Do not let the adhesive dry as it is difficult to remove and wall tile adhesive dries quite quickly.

13 Complete all the full tiles before cutting the edge tiles or any tiles around fittings such as taps and pipes (see Cutting ceramic tiles, pages 140–2). Butter the back of the edge

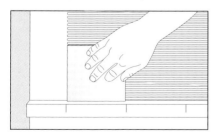

8 Start the tiling in one corner along the bottom batten. Leave the corner tiles until last.

tiles with enough adhesive to ensure they are aligned with adjacent full tiles. Repeat for each tile up the wall.

14 Once the tiles above the batten are laid and set, remove the batten to allow the bottom row of tiles to be fixed. If the floor is level, little, if any, trimming of tiles will be required. Each of these tiles is buttered in a similar way to edge tiles and fixed in place, ensuring they are aligned with the tiles above.

15 Allow the adhesive to dry for 24 hours before grouting. After this time, attach ceramic accessories such as soap holders, toilet roll holders and towel rail ends. Apply the adhesive to the back of the fitting and set in place. Use masking tape to hold the fitting in place while the adhesive sets.

GROUTING

16 Fill the joints between tiles with a compressible grouting material. Mix the grout according to the instructions on the package. Add the grout to water and mix to produce a smooth paste that will hold its shape.

17 Apply the grout with a rubber squeegee. Work the grout well into the joints to completely fill them. Working diagonally across the joints will avoid digging the grout out behind the squeegee as you pass over a joint. As the grout is being worked in, use the rubber edge to keep the face of the tiles clean. There should be very little waste.

18 Neaten and further compress the grout into the joint using a 6–10 mm timber dowel. Always draw the dowel towards you as pushing it away may dislodge the grout.

19 When completed, wipe the excess grout off the wall using a damp cloth or sponge. Wash the grout out of the sponge frequently. The result is a wall that is clean and has just a hint of grout left on the tile surface.

20 Allow the grout to dry for 24 hours and polish the surface with a soft cloth or crumpled newspaper. This will remove any grout left on the surface and give a shine.

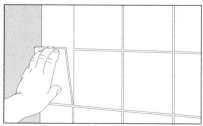

13 Individually butter the edge tiles with adhesive and press them into place on the wall.

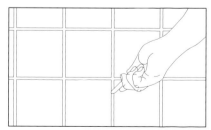

18 Draw a timber dowel slowly along the grouted joints to neaten and compress the grout.

Coloured grouts such as the green grout used in this tiled wall look particularly effective when the tiling is all in one colour. The brighter green of the grout complements the softer tones of the tiles.

Tiling a kitchen splashback is an easy project for beginners. Avoid tiles that appear porous or those with a textured surface as the area will need to be constantly wiped.

Kitchen splashback

Brighten your kitchen with this beautiful chequerboard splashback using sunny yellow and white ceramic tiles.

PREPARATION

1 The preparation of the surface and methods and materials used are the same as for Tiling a wall, pages 170–7. This splashback is 400 mm high and takes four 100 mm tiles, but the size will depend on your kitchen.

2 Decide whether you want to centre a grout joint or a tile directly behind the spout of the kitchen tap, or the central divider between the two sink bowls.

3 Check that your worktop is level with a spirit level. You can then tile directly from the worktop making an allowance (using spacer crosses) for a sealant between the tiles and the benchtop. The silicone allows for the movement between the tiles and the kitchen worktop. Adjust the layout of the tiles around any obstruction to avoid excessive tile cutting.

FIXING THE TILES

4 Apply a thin bed of adhesive to the wall as per the manufacturer's recommendations. Form the gap to the worktop by temporarily laying down a row of spacer crosses or matchsticks along the wall, using two spacer crosses per tile. Allow a 2 mm space between the tiles or use spacer crosses. Pay special attention to joints as the bright tiles accentuate any inaccuracies.

5 Grout the tiles, but leave the bottom joint between the worktop and the tiles clear. If grout gets into the joint clear it out with a knife before it sets. Leave the grout to dry for 24 hours before polishing.

6 Fill the joint to the worktop with a pigmented silicone sealant to match the grout colour. Clear silicone will tend to show mould growth.

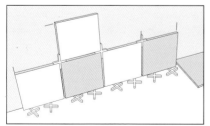

3 Using spacers under the tiles, set out the tiles along the wall without adhesive to find the best arrangement.

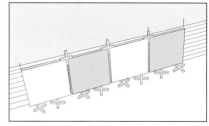

4 Apply the adhesive with the grooves running horizontally and install the tiles on the spacer crosses.

Tiled frieze

Add interest to a plain tiled wall by inserting a frieze of border tiles. Tiling a frieze is similar to normal wall tiling. The only variation is setting out the wall to allow for the different sizes of the frieze and border tiles. This frieze was created using small square and triangular tiles. Tile suppliers can also cut tiles to shape.

PREPARATION

1 Start by laying out the design on a horizontal surface. Use spacer crosses to give the right grout joints between the tiles. First lay out the number of body tiles up to the frieze level and then lay out the small tile pieces in the design you want.

2 Measure the height of each course of tiles, including the body tiles, and write them down. Measure the complete height of the frieze design and note that measurement. The rest of the wall will fall into place.

3 If there are slight variations in the length of the frieze tiles compared to the size of the body tiles, try a variety of layout designs to find the best

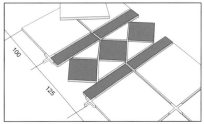

2 On a horizontal surface, measure the height of the tiles, including the body tiles, and write them down.

spacing of joints – decide whether to off-set the joints or line them up.

4 Transfer the measurements to the wall, measuring from the lowest part of the floor. Draw level lines around the room or along the wall to define the top and bottom of the frieze area.

LAYING THE TILES

5 Lay the bottom courses of body tiles up to the frieze level including the cut tiles at the edges.

6 Apply adhesive for the frieze and fix the tiles. Take care not to push the tiny tiles into the adhesive too hard. Use a wood block to press them into the adhesive. If the tiles tend to creep down the wall, use the end of a spacer cross or a matchstick to hold them in place until the adhesive has dried.

7 Clean any excess adhesive from between the tiles as you work. Continue laying the rest of the tiles.

8 Allow the adhesive to dry. Grout and clean as for normal ceramic tiling (see Grouting, page 176).

When choosing tiles for a frieze, select ones that are the same size or totally different from the wall tiles. Tiles that are nearly the same size are difficult to incorporate into a design successfully.

Timber framed tile frieze

A dado or feature chair rail makes a very attractive feature in a traditional dining, sitting or lounge room. The border can be further enhanced by adding a tiled frieze between polished timber battens.

PREPARATION

1 The preparation of the surface, and tiling methods and materials used are described on pages 170–7.

2 Decide on the layout of the rebated timber edging and how you want to set out the frieze. There are two options:

• Fix the tiles directly to the wall, adding an attractive timber moulding above and below.

• Set out the moulding and add a backing board to raise the relief from the wall (as used for this project).

LAYING THE TILES

3 Cut a strip of MDF, plywood or chipboard the height of the chosen tile, adding allowance for the grout and the rebate in the timber

surround. Nail or screw this to the wall, using a spirit level to ensure it is horizontal.

4 For this timber framed frieze we cut a moulding from 38 x 19 mm timber using a router with a beading bit to produce the shape. The bottom edge is finished with 19 mm maple scotia. Fill nail holes, sand smooth and paint with two coats of clear polyurethane.

5 Set out the tiles to find the best spacing and pattern, and mark the position of the joints on the strip.

6 Apply wall tile adhesive to the back of individual tiles and press them on to the strip with a slight twisting motion. Keep the joint spacing even at about 1 mm.

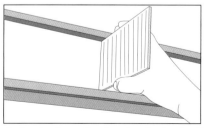

6 Apply the adhesive to the back of the tile to avoid smearing the adhesive on the timber work.

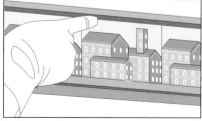

7 Apply the grout by hand and avoid smearing grout all over the work, especially over the wood.

These hand-painted ceramic tiles look effective when framed by timber moulding. This moulding has been routed to produce the shape but there are some suitable moulded timbers available that are rebated to accommodate the tiles.

7 Allow the adhesive to set overnight then grout the joints. As the area is very narrow mix the grout a little thicker than normal. Wearing a rubber glove, apply the grout using your finger. Try to avoid smearing the grout on the timber work. Grout a metre or two at a time and clean off the excess grout with a wrung-out sponge and many changes of water. Pay special attention to removing the grout from the timber grain.

8 After 24 hours polish the surface with a soft cloth or newspaper. Apply a final coat of finish to the timber, making sure you do not paint on to the surface of the tile.

This colourful tiled panel is made using a rigid backing of chipboard. A reverse bevelled edge at the top creates a convenient hanging system, allowing the panel to be moved.

Tiled panel

A wall panel of ceramic tiles can add a bright splash of colour just about anywhere. This panel is composed of 100 mm handmade and hand-painted tiles in an abstract pattern of various colours.

METHOD

1 Decide on the size of the panel and choose tiles you like. Tiles are quite heavy so don't make it too big. Make the panel a multiple of the tile size.

2 Using a circular saw, cut a 50 x 19 mm batten lengthways at an angle of about 15 degrees. Glue and screw one part to the top of the rear of the panel with the angled cut at the bottom. Retain the offcut. Write 'top' on the front of the panel.

3 Set out the tiles. In this case, there are many shades of colour, so write the colour on the back of the tiles and draw a plan of their location. As the tiles vary in size slightly, draw a grid of the tiles on the panel.

4 If the panel you are intending to tile is unlikely to get wet, the tiles may be glued to the panel with a construction adhesive that is suitable for both timber and ceramic. The adhesive remains slightly flexible and is a non-messy option for small projects. If the panel is likely to come in contact with water, a premixed ceramic tile adhesive and a sealed board should be used, as would be normal for wall tiling.

Apply four dobs of adhesive on the back of the tiles and locate each tile centrally in its square and gently press it in place.

5 Let the adhesive set for 24 hours. Prepare a 63 x 12 mm hardwood frame and paint it black with an oil-based paint. Mitre the corners and glue and nail the edging in place.

6 Allow the paint to dry and grout the tiles. A coloured grout is suitable here: grey was used for this project. Be careful when using coloured grouts as some tiles can absorb the grout into the fine crazing, so try the grout on a spare tile first.

7 Screw the angled batten offcut to the wall studs or brickwork and lift the panel into place.

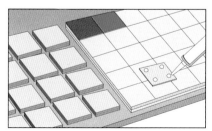

4 Apply four dobs of adhesive on the back of the tile and glue it on to the panel.

Mosaic tiles are bought as sheets that are either backed by netting or, occasionally, paper facing. Mosaic tiles are not difficult to lay — their mesh backing allows them to stretch or compress to fit the surface.

Tiling with sheet tiles

Small tiles, sometimes known as mosaic tiles, are sold in sheets with a mesh or paper backing and can be used on walls or floors. Often made of ceramic material but sometimes of glass or marble, the laying procedure is simple.

TILING THE FLOOR WITH MOSAICS

1 Prepare the floor for tiling and set it out in a similar manner to tiling with larger tiles. Adjust the starting point to minimise the need for cut tiles – stretch or compress the grout joints. Cut the sections of tile sheets by cutting through the backing.

2 Only work on one quarter of the surface at a time. To keep the tiles in line, mark off the floor as a grid to act as a constant reference where each tile sheet should start and finish.

3 Apply the adhesive with a 6 mm notched trowel. The adhesive for floor mosaics should be slightly drier than the adhesive used for larger tiles as it is very easy to press individual

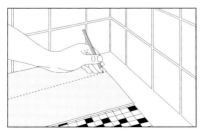

1 Place the sheet of mosaic tiles upside down and mark on the back of the net where the cuts are needed.

TOOLS
• Tape measure
• Spirit level and straight-edge
• Plumb line
• 6 mm notched trowel
• Buckets (several) for mixing adhesive and water
• Spatula
• Sponges or scourers
• Rubber squeegee (for applying grout)
• Tile pincers

tiles into soft adhesive, resulting in an uneven floor. Another reason is that as you adjust the tiles, water tends to rise to the surface and may make it difficult to bed the tile evenly.

4 Lay the tiles to the grid marked on the floor. Press the tiles into place using a flat piece of timber (about 250 x 100 mm). Align any tiles that are skewed as you work. Be careful not to work yourself into a corner.

5 Cut the edge sheets as you work – you may not be able to reach them after a large segment of the tiling is completed. Use tile pincers to cut around floor wastes and drain pipes.

6 Clean off any excess adhesive from the face of the tiling using a slightly damp sponge and several changes of water. Do not use a wet sponge as the water will be added to the adhesive and will make the bedding too soft. It is very hard to adjust mosaic tiles in soft bedding as they tend to 'sink'.

7 Allow the adhesive to dry for at least 24 hours and grout the floor using floor grout or the tile adhesive (see Grouting, page 155). The floor will take light traffic once the tiles have been polished.

TILING THE WALLS
8 Prepare the surface for tiling (see Tiling a wall 1, page 171).

9 Hold a sheet of tiles against the wall where it appears to be the lowest point. Mark the top of the sheet and using a spirit level draw a horizontal line around the room. If there is a point where the floor is more than a few millimetres lower than your starting point, adjust the line down.

10 Mark a vertical line in the middle of the wall as a starting point. Set out the spacing of tile sheets along the wall so you have full tiles in each corner. Cut the netting between the tiles to give you the required number of tiles. As there is some flexibility in the tile sheets, the grout joints of the last two sheets can be stretched or compressed as necessary to fit neatly into the corner of the wall. Normally, small mosaic tiles do not require cutting into the corner but if the mosaics are over 25 mm, cutting may be required. Mark where each sheet of tiles is to be located on the horizontal line. Hold a tile sheet above the horizontal line so there is a slight grout gap below the sheet and mark a second horizontal line.

LAYING THE MOSAICS
11 Starting at the vertical line, apply adhesive to the space between the lines. Use a 6 mm notched trowel to spread the adhesive and finish by ribbing the adhesive horizontally.

12 Position the first sheet of tiles and align the joints accurately. Press the

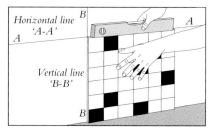

10 Starting from a vertical (B–B), mark where each sheet of tiles is to be located on the horizontal line (A–A).

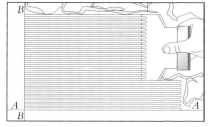

11 Apply the adhesive to the wall and then use a 6 mm notched trowel to rib the adhesive horizontally.

tiles into place using a flat piece of timber to bed them into the adhesive. Run your hand over the tiles to make sure the surface feels even. If the tiles are heavy and the adhesive is soft, the netting could stretch a little when it is wet with the adhesive and will sag. To prevent this, temporarily nail some small tacks under a few of the tiles in the top row to hold them in place until the adhesive has set.

13 Continue tiling into the corner, making sure that the tile joints are evenly spaced and the top of the row remains horizontal. Compress or expand grout joints as necessary in the last two tile sheets to fit the corner.

14 Leave cut tiles until all full tiles have been laid. If there is insufficient space to apply adhesive in a corner, butter the back of the sheets. Tile the column on the other side of the vertical line to complete one row on the wall.

15 Mark the next row in a similar way and continue working up the wall to reach the required level.

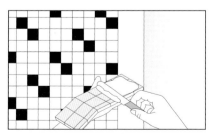

14 Butter the back of the mosaic tile sheets if there is insufficient space in the corner to use a trowel.

16 When the tiling above the marked bottom line (see step 9, page 188) is finished, fit the bottom row of sheets. If there is a little variation in the level of the floor, compress the tile sheets to give slightly narrow grout joints at this level. Do not close up the grout joints to less than 1 mm as the grout will not penetrate the joint effectively. If necessary, pull the mosaic tiles off the netting and carefully nip off the unwanted part with pincers.

17 Wipe off any excess adhesive with a damp cloth, being careful not to push the mosaic tiles out of alignment. Let the adhesive set for 24 hours and then grout the joints as for normal ceramic tiling (see Grouting, page 155).

TILING CURVED SURFACES WITH MOSAICS

Mosaic tile is the ideal material to tile both convex and concave surfaces. As with wall tiling the starting point is one tile sheet above the floor level. Mark out a series of true vertical lines to keep the tiles in alignment. Apply the adhesive with a 6 mm notched trowel. Press the tiles in place using a narrow strip of timber held vertically. If possible, cut a template of the curve using a 600 mm wide piece of plywood to check your progress and to align the tiles evenly in the curve.

Terracotta tile paving

Lay paving tiles on a reinforced concrete base. Pour the slab well before your paving project is scheduled to begin, as newly poured concrete requires adequate curing time.

TOOLS

- Basic tool kit (see page 75)
- 10 mm notched trowel
- Bolt cutters or angle grinder
- Rubber squeegee
- Rubber gloves
- Sponges
- Pliers
- Buckets
- Chalk string
- Tile pincers
- Builders square
- Wooden float
- Tile cutter, brick saw or angle grinder with diamond blade

PREPARATION

1 Mark out the area, allowing for sufficient fall. Consider whether the dimensions accommodate full tiles.

2 Set finished height stringlines.

3 Excavate to a depth of 120 mm.

4 Use 100 x 50 mm timber to form up the area. Nail the formwork to pegs positioned outside the rails.

5 Prepare the concrete slab, making sure it is level and flat.

6 Finish the surface with a wooden float to create a slightly rough texture. Neaten with an edging tool.

7 Keep the slab moist for five to seven days. Hose it down gently with

MATERIALS

- 100 x 50 mm rails for formwork
- Concrete
- A142M steel mesh and ties
- Mesh men
- Terracotta tiles 280 mm square
- Tile adhesive
- Tile grout
- Acid for etching

water, then cover it completely with plastic. Allow adequate time for thorough curing.

CHOOSING AN ADHESIVE

8 Choose a flexible adhesive for strength, or mix a mortar of three parts sand to one part cement for ease of spreading or to disguise undulations in the concrete base.

Contrasting border inlays break up large expanses of terracotta tiles and can be used to reflect the colour scheme of nearby paintwork or plantings. Patient planning is necessary when calculating a detailed design.

A simple chequerboard pattern in blue and white offsets the rich rusty tone of this terracotta-tiled porch.

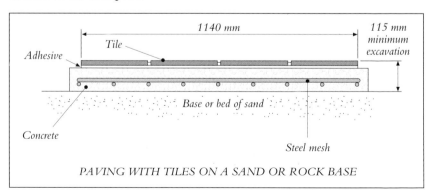

1140 mm

115 mm minimum excavation

Tile

Adhesive

Base or bed of sand

Concrete

Steel mesh

PAVING WITH TILES ON A SAND OR ROCK BASE

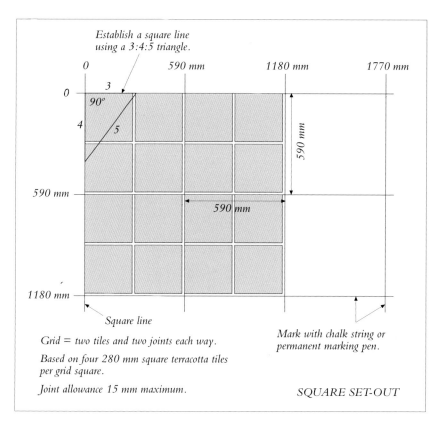

Establish a square line
using a 3:4:5 triangle.

0   590 mm   1180 mm   1770 mm

0   3
       90°
4   5

590 mm

590 mm

590 mm

1180 mm

Square line

Grid = two tiles and two joints each way.

Based on four 280 mm square terracotta tiles
per grid square.

Joint allowance 15 mm maximum.

Mark with chalk string or
permanent marking pen.

SQUARE SET-OUT

Lay the adhesive to a uniform depth. If the slab is level, create fall by graduating the adhesive or mortar from 30–40 mm to 10–20 mm.

SETTING OUT

9 Lay out the tiles to check that your selected pattern is possible with minimal cutting. Thin slivers of tile are difficult to cut, so adjust the joints to correct the set-up.

Choose from two design options.

• For a square set-out (see Square set-out, above), measure the spacing of two standard paving tiles and their

corresponding joints to determine the grid, then transfer this on to the base. Stretch a chalk string between the grid points and flick it to mark

HINT

Terracotta tiles are surprisingly porous, so soak them in water for between twenty and thirty minutes (as recommended by the manufacturer) before laying. Dry tiles act like sponges, sucking moisture from the adhesive and weakening the paving bond.

the concrete surface. Draw a 3:4:5 triangle in one corner to create a 90 degree angle. Measure the grid spacing in the opposite direction on both sides and continue marking. The time spent setting out a grid simplifies the laying process and saves unnecessary cutting, so work carefully to ensure your preferred pattern is achievable.

• To create a diagonal set-out (see Diagonal set-out, page 195), begin by laying a header course of, for example, rectangular half-tiles. Use a builders square or measure a 3:4:5 triangle to ascertain that the first corner is square, so that the cuts required down the sides will not vary. Using a platform tile cutter, angle grinder or diamond-blade saw, cut several tiles into diagonal quarters and halves. Use a quarter-tile in one corner as the basis of your pattern. Establish that the area is square and mark a diagonal line from the back of the first corner tile. Draw this line as a 3:4:5 triangle and mark it in chalk. Mark a diagonal line perpendicular to

HINT

Freshly laid concrete must be allowed to cure for several months before tiles or slate pavers are laid. The longer the curing time provided, the harder the finished base will be, with fewer cracks. As a rough guide, allowing at least one month for each 25 mm thickness of concrete is recommended.

the first, again based on a 3:4:5 triangle. Referring to these lines, continue ruling a 590 mm square grid. Lay out two rows then measure the spacing of two tiles and two joints each way to use as grid sizing.

CREATING A FIRM HOLD
10 Etch the slab with a mix of hydrochloric acid and water in a 1:10 ratio. (Always add the acid to the water – do not work in reverse). Spread the mix over the concrete and rub it firmly with a stiff-bristled broom. Rinse the slab with clean water and allow it to dry.

11 Work away from walls or other structures. To lay on the diagonal, start in one corner. Lay complete rows or cover one quarter at a time.

12 Mix sufficient tile adhesive for about 1 m^2 of tiles.

13 Using a metal float or bricklayer's trowel, spread adhesive onto the slab.

14 Use a 10–12 mm notched trowel held vertically to ridge the adhesive. Spread adhesive up to the grid lines.

LAYING THE TILES
15 Press each tile firmly onto the adhesive, twisting it slightly.

16 Tap the laid tiles gently with a rubber mallet to remove air bubbles. Continue tiling, leaving 10–12 mm gaps. Position the part-tiles as they occur, or cut them in bulk later.

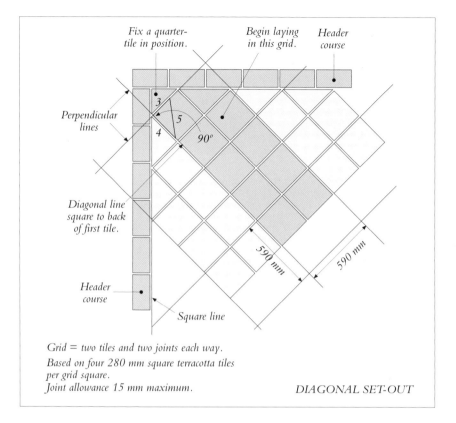

Fix a quarter-
tile in position.

Begin laying
in this grid.

Header
course

Perpendicular
lines

Diagonal line
square to back
of first tile.

Header
course

Square line

3

5

4

90°

590 mm

590 mm

Grid = two tiles and two joints each way.
Based on four 280 mm square terracotta tiles
per grid square.
Joint allowance 15 mm maximum.

DIAGONAL SET-OUT

17 Keep the surface of the tiles free of adhesive by cleaning them with a damp sponge as you work.

18 Use a straight-edge or spirit level to ensure the surface is even.

19 With a spirit level or straight-edge, check the horizontal lines, making minor adjustments to the surface if necessary.

20 Allow the adhesive to set, then grout the joints. Purchase pre-mixed grout from a tile retailer, or mix your own by using fine-grained sand and cement with water in a 4:1 ratio. Work on an area of approximately 1 m² at a time.

21 Using a rubber squeegee or heavy sponge, work the mixture into the joints. Remove extra grout from the tile face with a moistened sponge. Allow the grout to set.

22 Once the grout has dried, give the tiled surface a final clean down, again using a large, clean sponge dipped in fresh water.

Add impact to an area of plain tiling with this feature mosaic floor panel. Remember to check that the depth of the inset is the same as the depth of tiles (or other flooring material that you intend to use) so the finished floor is level.

Mosaic floor inset

This floor inset is made using the indirect method of applying mosaics. The tesserae are glued face down on a piece of brown paper and, when completed, transferred on to a waterproof board, which is inserted into the floor. This method ensures the surface of the inset is perfectly level.

<table>
<tr><td>

TOOLS

- Stylus (optional)
- Pencil
- Ruler
- Felt-tipped pen
- Goggles and mask
- Tile nippers
- Mixing containers
- Brush
- Rubber gloves
- Palette knife
- Small trowel
- Rubber squeegee
- Sponges
- Rags or cloths

</td><td>

MATERIALS

- Carbon paper (optional)
- 700 x 700 mm brown paper or craft paper
- 50 x 50 mm glass mosaic tesserae: cream, light green
- 20 x 20 mm glass mosaic tesserae: dark brown, maroon, cream, yellow, black, dark orange, caramel
- Wallpaper paste
- Multi-purpose tile adhesive
- 600 x 600 mm marine plywood or pre-sealed board

</td></tr>
</table>

PREPARATION

1 Use a photocopier to increase the the pattern for the floor inset to the correct size (page 200). Transfer the design on to a piece of brown paper using carbon paper and the stylus. If the pencilled lines are difficult to see on the brown paper, draw over them with a felt-tipped pen.

The design is 600 x 600 mm, but cut the brown paper larger than this so it is easier to handle when you have to transfer the tesserae off the paper on to the waterproof board.

Alternatively, as this is quite a basic design, you may find it easier to draw the design on the brown paper using a pencil and ruler, following the measurements on the pattern. Add in the flower motifs by hand.

2 Wearing goggles and a mask, cut enough tesserae to start work on one area. Start with the four green and white bands. These bands are made up of whole, large cream tesserae and light green tesserae, which are cut in half diagonally to form two triangles.

3 Following the manufacturer's directions, prepare a small amount of wallpaper paste.

FIXING THE TESSERAE

4 Using a brush, apply wallpaper paste to the brown paper, along one of the bands. Lay the uncut cream tesserae first, placing them upside down on the glue. Similarly, fix the half green tesserae in place. Complete all the bands in this manner.

5 Add crisscrossing lines of thin brown tesserae around these tiles. Remember to lay all the tiles upside down. Place a small maroon square at the point where the lines intersect.

6 Work on the central large flower. Using tile nippers, cut a circle from a small cream tessera and place it in the centre of the flower. Add a row of thin rectangular tesserae outlining the circle. Border this with a row of maroon. Fill in the petals with yellow.

7 Outline the black square with a border of thin, rectangular black tesserae. Fill in the area around the

yellow flower with randomly shaped pieces of black.

8 Add two rows of smaller cream tesserae around the black square. These tesserae are used whole. To each corner add an uncut dark orange tessera outlined by a border of black.

9 Fill in the four flowers on the outer corners with dark orange, and fill in the remaining area of the square with black.

10 Outline the cream and green bands with a single row of thin maroon tesserae. Fill in the outer border with caramel, worked in a basketweave pattern (see the photograph on page 199).

11 When the design is completed, allow the wallpaper adhesive to dry for 24 hours before transferring the tesserae to the waterproof board.

TRANSFERRING THE TESSERAE

12 Using a trowel, apply a thin, even bed of adhesive to the board.

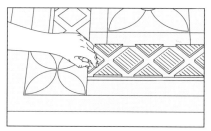

4 Apply wallpaper paste to one area at a time and place the tesserae upside down on the brown paper.

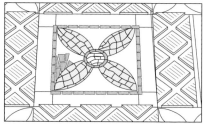

7 Position a row of black tesserae around the border of the square; fill in the remaining area.

CAUTION

When using the indirect method the tesserae are placed upside down on the paper. If you are using glass mosaic tesserae it is easy to see how the pattern is working (the back of the tesserae are coloured the same as the front), but if you are using ceramic tesserae, take extra care and follow the pattern carefully as the backs of these tiles are all clay coloured.

The edge of the inset is made up of a row of maroon, and a basketweave pattern made up of caramel tesserae.

13 Working quickly (but carefully) so that the adhesive does not dry out, lift the tiled design on the brown paper and turn it over on to the waterproof board, aligning the edges of the tiled design with the board. The back of the tesserae should be sitting in the adhesive and the brown paper should be facing upwards. Ensure the tiles are pressed evenly into the bed of adhesive. Allow the adhesive to dry for 24 hours.

14 Using a damp sponge and warm water, dampen the surface of the paper. The paper will easily peel off

the surface of the mosaic to reveal the design, right way up.

FINISHING

15 Using the rubber squeegee, apply the grey grout over the surface (see page 155). Wipe off the excess with the squeegee or use a cloth.

16 With a damp sponge, and rinsing regularly, wipe off the excess grout. When dry, polish the surface using a clean rag.

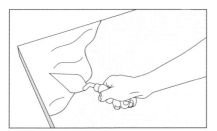

12 Using a small trowel, apply a thin bed of tile adhesive to the waterproof board.

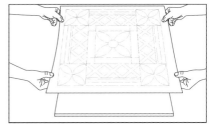

13 Lift the tesserae on the brown paper and place it on to the board with the paper facing upwards.

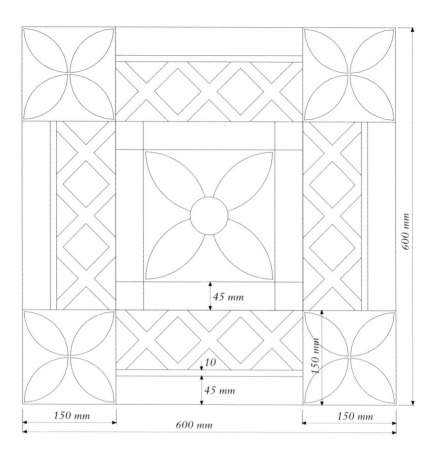

Floor inset (page 196)

Using a photocopier, enlarge the image by 600% (enlarge by 200%, then 200%, and then by 150%).

MAKING MOSAICS: THE DIRECT OR INDIRECT METHOD?

The size and shape of your mosaic will determine which method you use to complete it. The direct method is recommended for:
• mosaic murals, splashbacks and designs that use a lot of colour;
• work on surfaces that are uneven or three-dimensional.

The birdbath on page 203 is an example of mosaic using the direct method.

The disadvantage of the direct method is that if you are using various types of tesserae, the uneven thickness of the tesserae will give you an uneven finished surface.

The indirect method is recommended for:
• work that cannot be carried out directly on site;
• mosaics that require the finished surface to be perfectly flat, such as the floor mosaic on page 196;
• work on a detailed design that would otherwise be partly obscured by the adhesive when applying the direct method.

CLEANING MOSAICS

In some cases, it may be necessary to use a commercial tile cleaner or a diluted solution of hydrochloric acid to give your mosaic its final clean. This may be the case if you are using a cement-based adhesive, or if the grout has dried too much and it is difficult to remove from the surface of the tiles with soap and water. If the surface film of grout can't be removed with a cloth and water, try the following method using hydrochloric acid.

1 If possible, take the mosaic outside to be cleaned. Wear gloves and eye protection at all times when handling the hydrochloric acid. If there are any splashes, wash the affected area immediately with lots of water.
2 Add one part acid to fifteen parts of water in a bucket or container. Always add the acid to the water to minimize the chance of the acid splashing up and burning you.
3 Brush the acid solution over the mosaic and immediately wash it off with lots of clean water. It is important that no trace of acid be left on the mosaic.
4 Allow the surface of the mosaic to dry, then polish the mosaic using a soft cloth.

Birdbath

Larger projects, such as this colourful birdbath, may take two or three sittings to complete. The actual design is quite simple: what really makes this birdbath so effective is the use of bright colour and the varying angles at which the tesserae are laid.

TOOLS

- Brush for sealer
- Pencil
- Compass
- Stylus (optional)
- Tile nippers
- Goggles and mask
- Mixing containers
- Palette knife
- Rubber gloves
- Rubber squeegee
- Rags or cloths
- Sponges

MATERIALS

- Concrete birdbath (with dish and stand in separate pieces)
- Waterproof sealer for concrete
- Cement-based tile adhesive
- Old china or crockery: assorted patterns
- Glass mosaic tesserae: yellow, purple, red, light blue, bronze, turquoise, dark blue
- Black grout

PREPARATION

1 Seal all the surfaces of the birdbath (both sides of the dish and the stand) with concrete waterproofing sealer and allow it to dry.

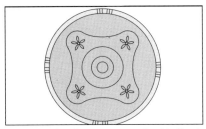

2 Draw the design on to the birdbath using a pencil. Draw three circles, the floral shape and the four flowers.

2 As the design for the birdbath contains little detail, follow the illustration on the left and draw the design directly on to the birdbath. Start by locating the centre of the birdbath and draw three circles approximately 20 mm, 30 mm and 65 mm in diameter. You can use a compass to do this or a string and pencil (see page 156).

Add in the large floral shape around the outer circle, and the four small flowers in each of the corners. Draw in the detail on the four areas around the rim.

You do not need to draw a pattern for the birdbath stand as the design is worked to suit the shape of your particular stand.

When selecting your birdbath, choose one that is simple in design with as many smooth surfaces as possible. Too many curves and raised patterns will cause difficulties when you are trying to fix the tesserae in place.

The contours of your stand will determine the best way to mosaic it. Follow the photograph as a guide for tiling your own stand.

TILING THE DISH

3 Start working in the centre of the birdbath. Using tile nippers, cut a small circle from the patterned china. Fix it in the centre using adhesive. Surround this with a border of china tesserae to complete the first circle.

4 Add a row of yellow to complete the second circle.

5 Cut the purple tesserae into thin rectangular shapes and lay them around the yellow circle, radiating outwards. Surround this with a border of red and then light blue to complete the third circle.

6 Cut four small circles from the crockery and fix them in the centre

of each flower. For each flower, cut five petal shapes from the bronze tesserae. Butter the back of the tesserae with adhesive and fix in place.

7 Define the large floral shape by outlining it with thin rectangles of turquoise. Fill inside this area with random shapes of turquoise and outline with a row of yellow.

8 Place a row of thin rectangles of dark blue around the yellow. Fill in the remaining area on the dish using randomly shaped blue tesserae.

9 Stick a row of whole blue tesserae around the inside rim. Apply the adhesive with a palette knife and allow it to dry for 10 minutes so the adhesive becomes slightly tacky. If it is wet, the tesserae will slide down the side. Position the uncut edge of the tesserae uppermost to make the finish neater. Allow the adhesive to set.

10 Turn the dish over and tile the back. Starting in the centre, stick a row of thin, red tesserae around the dish, followed by a row of light blue.

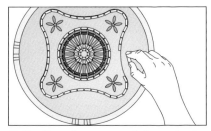

7 Outline the outer and inner border of the floral shape using rectangular turquoise tesserae.

Fill in with turquoise. The outside rim is tiled with purple. Allow to dry before turning it face up.

11 Tile the top of the rim. Start with the four detailed areas. Cut four small squares from crockery and fix them in place. Border these with red, then yellow tesserae cut into thin rectangles. Fill in around the rim with light blue tesserae.

TILING THE STAND
12 Cut the flowers from pieces of china and stick them randomly around the main section of the stand.

13 Fill in around the flowers using dark blue. Tile the rest of the stand using the photograph on page 204 as a guide. You may need to alter the tiling pattern slightly, depending on the size and shape of your stand.

FINISHING
14 Allow 24 hours for the adhesive to dry. Wearing gloves, spread the black grout over the surface of the birdbath. Wipe off the excess with a rag (see Grouting, page 155).

Don't forget to mosaic the back of the dish. Choose two or three colours and fix them in bands around the dish.

15 Allow the grout to dry; turn the dish over and repeat the process to grout the back. While the dish is drying, grout the stand.

16 Once dry, give the birdbath a final polish with a rag to remove any grout residue. Allow at least 72 hours for curing before using the birdbath.

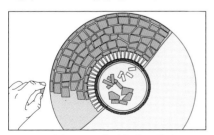

10 Working on half the dish at a time, apply the tesserae to the back of the dish.

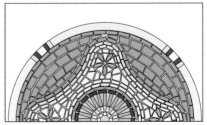

11 Use small squares of crockery and red and yellow tesserae and place them on four points around the rim.

Tiling a worktop

Tiling a worktop is not difficult, but it does need more care than tiling a wall and you need to choose the correct materials to ensure the worktop will last.

- Tape measure
- Hammer and nails
- Screwdriver and screws
- Saw
- Notched adhesive spreader
- Timber straight-edge
- Tile cutting machine
- Filling knife
- Kitchen scouring pad
- Timber batten
- Hardboard spacers
- Masking tape

WORKTOP TILING

Tiles are a good way of giving an existing worktop a new lease of life, but it is better to start with a completely new surface, made from exterior (marine) grade plywood at least 12 mm thick. If possible, try to make this an exact number of tiles in width and length (allowing for grouting gaps) to avoid the need for tile cutting.

The tiles themselves should either be special 'worktop' tiles or the thicker ceramic floor tiles; do not use thin ceramic wall tiles which will be likely to crack. Unglazed or matt finish tiles are best for worktops.

ADHESIVES AND GROUTS

A normal (waterproof) tile adhesive can be used for fixing worktop tiles, but the grout must be a special two-part epoxy grout, which is tough, waterproof, resists stains and will not harbour germs. It is available in various colours.

PREPARATION

Cut the worktop to size and make any cut-outs for sinks or hobs. Sand the surface to be tiled and remove all the dust before screwing the worktop securely to the cupboards underneath.

SETTING OUT

1 If you have to cut tiles to fit either the length or the width, ensure that the cut tiles are against the wall or walls and at 'open' ends (i.e. those not against a wall). On a worktop with two open ends, you start tiling in the centre; if the worktop is in a corner, you start at the opposite corner; for an L-shaped worktop, start tiling at the inner (non-wall) corner where the two surfaces meet and work out in both directions.

2 Pin a temporary batten along the front of the worktop to act as a guide for laying the tiles.

A tiled worktop will enhance any kitchen, especially if you can match the tiles with those used on the wall. A painted timber trim protects the tile edges, but you could also use cap tiles.

FIXING THE TILES

3 Starting in the centre or at the corner (see Setting out on page 206), spread adhesive on the worktop using a notched applicator, covering no more than around 1 m² at a time.

4 Lay the tiles firmly on to the adhesive with pieces of hardboard between them to act as spacers. It is essential there are no air gaps underneath the tiles, so make sure you press them down firmly with a slight twisting action.

5 Check regularly with a spirit level or timber straight-edge that the tile surface is level. Lift any that are too high or too low and replace, using fresh adhesive.

6 Cut the edge tiles and put them in place, spreading adhesive on the back of the tile rather than on the worktop. Clean all adhesive off the face of the tiles and leave them to dry for 24 hours.

7 Remove the temporary battens and cut the hardwood moulding to size (with mitre joints at the corners) before gluing and screwing this to the worktop core material. Apply masking tape so that the moulding does not get damaged during the grouting process.

8 Mix up the grout and apply it using a filling knife, pressing the grout well into the gaps. Do not use grout in the gap between the worktop and wall.

9 Clean the whole surface with a kitchen scouring pad held flat so that it does not pull the grout out of the gaps. Wipe down and leave to dry.

10 When the grout has dried, give the surface a final polish, fill the gap between the worktop and the wall with a matching silicone sealant and remove the masking tape from the beading.

11 Fill the screw holes in the moulding and apply paint or varnish, this time masking the finished tiles. Remove the tape when the finish has dried.

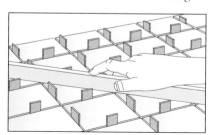

5 *When laying the tiles, check regularly with a spirit level or straight-edge that they are all at the same level.*

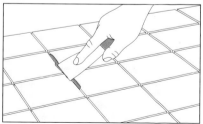

8 *With a filling knife, apply the two-part epoxy grout, pressing it well into the gap.*

Tools for tiling

Some of the most useful tools for tiling are shown below. Build up your tool kit gradually – most of the tools can be purchased from your local hardware or tiling store.

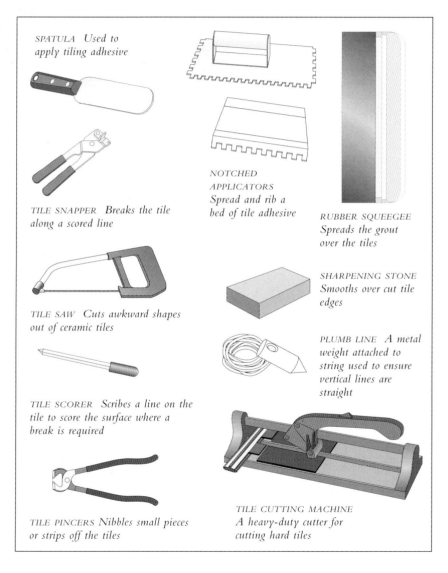

SPATULA *Used to apply tiling adhesive*

TILE SNAPPER *Breaks the tile along a scored line*

NOTCHED APPLICATORS *Spread and rib a bed of tile adhesive*

RUBBER SQUEEGEE *Spreads the grout over the tiles*

TILE SAW *Cuts awkward shapes out of ceramic tiles*

SHARPENING STONE *Smooths over cut tile edges*

TILE SCORER *Scribes a line on the tile to score the surface where a break is required*

PLUMB LINE *A metal weight attached to string used to ensure vertical lines are straight*

TILE PINCERS *Nibbles small pieces or strips off the tiles*

TILE CUTTING MACHINE *A heavy-duty cutter for cutting hard tiles*

Useful terms

aggregate crushed granite or basalt stone used in concrete and available in different screeded sizes, the largest being 20 mm

base material finely crushed gravel that compresses to a hard, solid base when compacted

bat a half or part brick

bed joint mortar joint between courses of bricks

bedding sand coarse-grained sand, such as washed river sand, from which all traces of salt and organic matter have been removed

bond geometric formation of bricks into a specific pattern

bonding agent substance used to improve the strength of adhesion between two surfaces

butter use trowel to put mortar on a brick before laying it

chipboard a panel made of wood chips, also known as particle board

commons bricks for internal work

creosote wood preservative that is obtained from the distillation of coal tar

cross joint vertical joint between bricks in a wall

curing process of initially keeping a concrete slab wet to increase strength and prevent cracking

direct method technique for laying mosaics in which the tesserae are glued directly on the surface. This is the preferred method when working on three-dimensional surfaces

drummy a term used to describe the hollow, drum-like sounds of poorly adhered tiles or render

efflorescence deposits of salt that appear on the surface of some paving materials

facing brick brick used for external or exposed brickwork

flashing in tiling, a plastic water barrier that is placed between adjacent tiled surfaces

footings concrete base structure

formwork removable timber frame used to contain a wet concrete slab

grout mixture of fine sand and cement used for filling joints in tiles and other paving surfaces

header brick that is set through the wall

header course border of bricks, usually laid side by side, to give strength to the edge of a path

indirect method in mosaics, method in which the tesserae are temporarily glued face down on paper and then transferred, right way up, on to a permanent base

lug projection on the sides or backs of tiles to aid in spacing or to provide grip for the adhesive

mortar mix of sand, cement and water, used to bond bricks or stones, or to give strength to a path

perpend cross joint

plumb vertical

polyurethane varnish a durable, clear coating for timber, cork or vinyl that is easily cleaned

profile frame set at the corners of a project; string lines attached to it to guide the worker

rack out step out the brickwork

resilient floor tiles tiles made from flexible PVC, linoleum, cork or rubber

screeding process of dragging back sand or mortar to a level finish prior to laying paving material

slurry wet mix of six parts cement to one part sand and water, often used to improve the bonding between the surface and the pavers

stretcher brick set along a wall

tessellating interlocking pattern that leaves no gaps

tessera 'tessera' (a single unit) and 'tesserae' (more than one) are derived from the Greek, meaning 'four', and refer to the four-cornered pieces originally used in mosaics. The term is used to describe a piece of pottery, glass or tile cut into a square, rectangle or triangle

vitrified highly fired ceramic material that has a high glass content and low porosity

weep hole opening in the mortar joint so water can escape

Index

Published by Murdoch Books UK Ltd
Ferry House, 51–57 Lacy Road, Putney,
London SW15 1PR

Murdoch Books® is a subsidiary of Murdoch Magazines Pty Ltd.
ISBN 1-85391-206-9
A catalogue record for this book is available from the British Library.
Managing Editor: Diana Hill
Editors: Christine Eslick, Melody Lord, Kim Rowney
Design Concept: Marylouise Brammer
Designers: Michèle Chan, Michelle Cutler, Wing Ping Tong
Photography: Andre Martin (pp. 60, 99, 105, 121, 123, 125, 129, 132, 134, 153, 186), Joe
Filshie (pp. 60, 126, 196, 199, 203, 204, 205), Tony Lyon (pp. 62, 66, 68, 74, 84, 89, 90, 95, 97,
109, 113, 116, 191, 192), Mil Truscott (pp. 6, 15, 19, 23, 25, 27, 29, 31, 34, 39, 41, 45, 47, 57),
Lorna Rose (pp. 103, 106)
Stylists: Kathy Tripp (all except specified), Georgina Dolling (p. 203), Louise Owens (pp. 132,
134, 136–8, 153, 186), Anna-Marie Bruechert (pp. 62, 66, 68, 74, 84, 89, 90, 95, 97, 109, 113,
116, 191, 192)
Illustrations: Stephen Pollitt
Authors: John Street (pp. 6–59), Frank Gardner (pp. 62–97, 108–18, 190–5), Dieter Mylius (pp.
132–89), Sabina Robba (pp. 196–205)
UK consultant: Ian Kearey
Production Manager: Lucy Byrne
CEO: Robert Oerton
Publisher: Catie Ziller
Group General Manager: Mark Smith

Do-It-Yourself Handbook *Bricks, Pavers & Tiles* has been compiled from the Mini Workbooks
Basic Brickwork Techniques & Projects, Planning & Building Paths, A Practical Guide to Paving, Tiling
and *Mosaics*

Produced by Phoenix Offset. PRINTED IN CHINA. First published in the UK in 2001.